GAME DEVELOPMENT GUIDE
PIXELPAD

PLATFORMER WORKBOOK

Copyright © 2022 by PixelPAD

Third Edition v3.1.0

EDITORS
Jamie Chang
Ivo van der Marel
Arthur Teles
Rochelle Magnaye

DESIGNERS
Fernando Medrano
Kenneth Chui
Prateeba Perumal
Emily Chow

www.pixelpad.io
www.underthegui.com

The Platformer Game Development Guide is part of the
Python Game Guide Series from PixelPAD.

Support us by getting more books from Amazon!

Our books are available on Amazon, search for:

PixelPAD Python

CONTENTS

COURSE GOALS & LEARNING OUTCOMES / 07

CHAPTER 01.
/ 09
- Setting Up

CHAPTER 02.
/ 12
- The Background
- The Player
- Moving The Player

CHAPTER 03.
/ 24
- The Enemy

CHAPTER 04.
/ 29
- Player Controls
- Player Directions
- The Platform

CHAPTER 05.
/ 38
- Gravity
- Collisions
- Jumping

CHAPTER 06.
/ 45
- Enemy Movement
- Colliding with Enemies

CHAPTER 07.
/ 52
- Shooting Projectile

CHAPTER 08.
/ 59
- Rooms

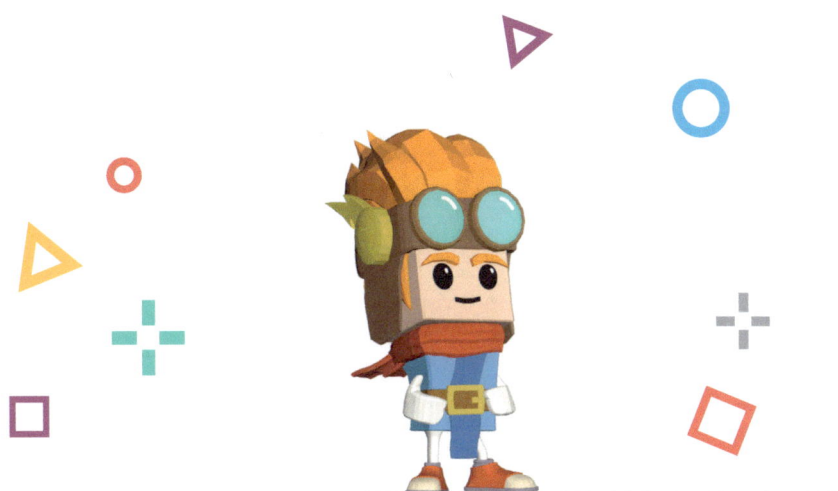

CHAPTER 09.

/ 73
- Enemy AI
- Health
- Enemy Health
- Sharing My Game

EXTRA ACTIVITIES	/ 81
GLOSSARY	/ 82
CHALLENGE QUESTION	/ 98
ERRORS GUIDE	/ 102

COURSE GOALS & LEARNING OUTCOMES

Students create a 2D Platformer game, and learn the basics of how to make a platformer. This will teach students simple physics concepts and how to implement it in their own games.

Similar to the Space Shooter game, students will be able to add features, change their sprites and personalize their game to make it uniquely their own. Additionally, they can continue to build on their game by creating more levels and customize their worlds using their creativity.

COURSE GOALS

- Students have an understanding of how to make different types of games and the ability to modify basic code to add new features to a game in PixelPAD
- Students finish with a full platforming game with challenges and multiple worlds

LEARNING OUTCOMES

Computational Thinking and Algorithms

- Students understand a simplified concept of gravity and how it affects objects
- Students can create their own variables and use them to customize gameplay
- Students can understand concepts related to physics, such as collision and speed
- Students understand and can describe concepts of object-oriented design and development in PixelPAD environment

Creativity

Students can generate custom worlds to challenge others through various puzzles.

Prototyping, Testing and Debugging

Students are able to read the Console and identify what line causes an error.

Construction

- Students can make a product in PixelPAD using known procedures or through modelling of others
- Student use trial and error to make changes, solve problems, or incorporate new ideas from self or others

Communication & Collaboration

- Students can demonstrate their product, tell the story of designing and making their product
- Students can use personal preferences to evaluate the success of their design solutions

SAMPLE PROJECT

The book's project can be found here:

https://pixelpad.io/app/htxurkcxtht/?edit=1

01.
CHAPTER

SETTING UP

In this workbook we will be making a 2D Platformer game where you will jump from one platform to another while avoiding enemies that appear along the way!

First, we will need to create a new project in pixelPAD. Once you've logged in you want to:

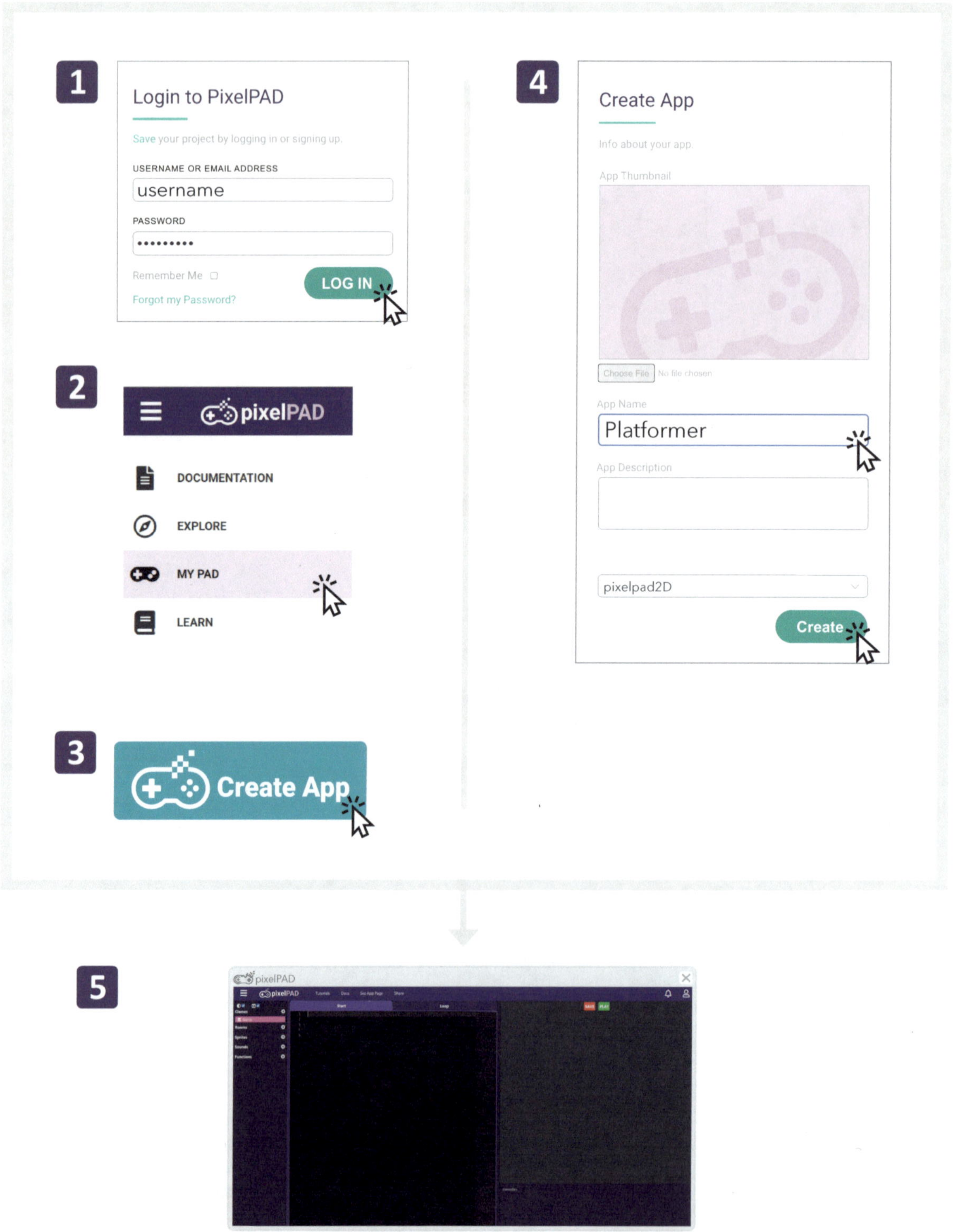

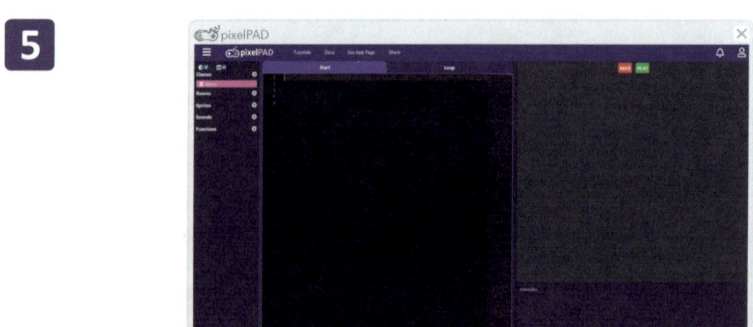

Once you created your project, you should see the PixelPAD Development Environment page.

PIXELPAD DEVELOPMENT ENVIRONMENT OVERVIEW

Classes, Rooms, Sprites, Sounds will appear here.

You can SAVE and PLAY your game with these buttons.

The Start and Loop tab can be clicked on here.

This is where your Game screen will appear when you click Play.

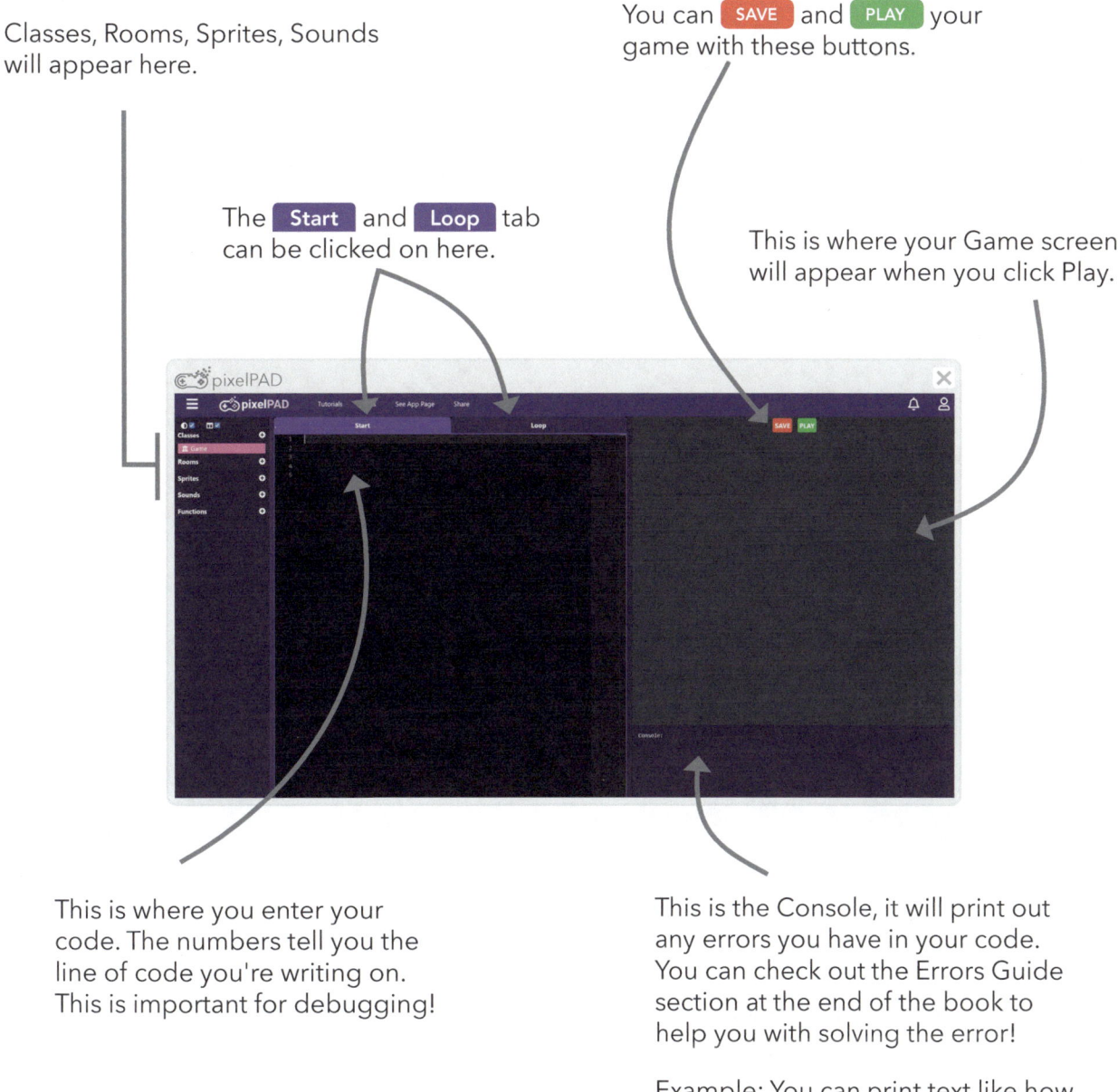

This is where you enter your code. The numbers tell you the line of code you're writing on. This is important for debugging!

This is the Console, it will print out any errors you have in your code. You can check out the Errors Guide section at the end of the book to help you with solving the error!

Example: You can print text like how many lives you have here.

02.
CHAPTER

THE BACKGROUND

Our game right now is totally empty. Let's add the simplest first: Our background!

A background will make our game look nicer. It is simply an image that is placed at the back of our game.

The first step is to create our **Background Class** by clicking on the white plus icon ⊕ next to the Classes menu.

1

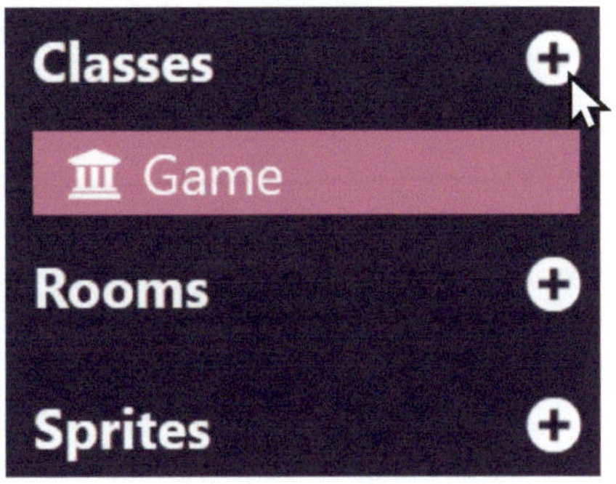

Then, a window will pop up asking us to give the Class a name. Name the Class Background, as shown below, and make sure to capitalize the "B" in Background. When you are done, click OK.

Capitalizing the first letter of a Class name is important because it helps distinguish Classes from regular variables (more on variables later).

2

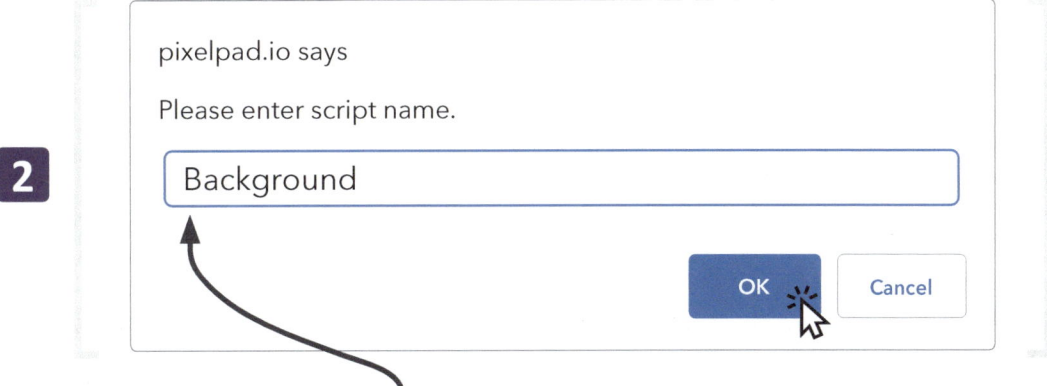

Again, make sure you **capitalize** the "B" in Background as shown.

You should now see the Background Class you just created right below the Game Class. The pink highlight means you have opened that Class. In this image, the Game Class is open.

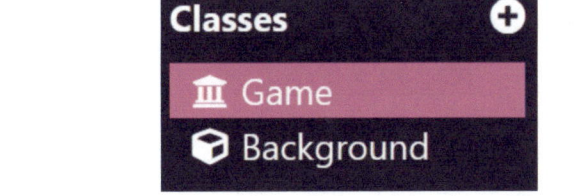

Now, we will add some code that will make the background image appear on the screen!

3 Click on the 🏛 Game Class, then click on the Start Tab of your editor.

Pay attention to the pink and purple tabs here! These tell you where to type in your code.

Add the following **bolded code** below. Type it **exactly** as it's shown!

4

🏛 Game | Start

`self.coast = Background()`

This line of code creates something called a **variable**.

A variable is used to store some value, this one we named "coast". With it, we are storing an object of type "Background", using the command Background().

For in-depth explanation of the Start and Loop Tabs, head to the glossary section that explains The Game Loop!

5

SAVE + PLAY

Whenever you add content to your game it is a good idea to press the **RED SAVE** button at the top right of your game window! Then press **PLAY** to see the results of your code!

Notice how we've used the words classes and objects in this project so far. Don't be confused by them! A class is simply a blueprint that we use to construct/create the objects that we interact with in our game. For example, our Background class is the blueprint from which we create "actual" background objects such as our coast.

You may notice that your object shows up but it's a small blue box that says empty image... This is because we haven't assigned our object a **sprite**. In game development terms, an image is called a "sprite".

A **sprite** is a computer graphic that is moved on a screen or manipulated. Generally, sprites refer to 2D images that make up our game's art.

So for our Background object, we need to assign a sprite. To do this, first click on the ⊕ icon to the right of the Sprites menu.

6

This will open up the PixelPad's Asset Library, which will allow you to either select an existing sprite or upload one from your computer! You can click on the tabs on the left to select a category and click on Previous/Next to navigate the pages.

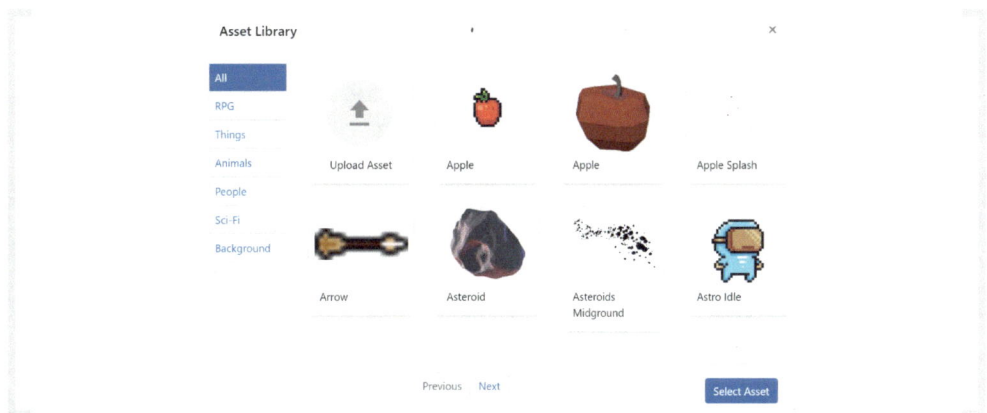

For our example, we will be using the Coast Background sprite. To select it, click on the background image, then click Select Asset

7

Note: If you've decided to upload a sprite from your computer, make sure it has a .png/.jpg extension at the end of the name.

Once you've selected/uploaded a background sprite that you like click on select asset. Now, a window will pop up asking you to give your sprite a name. Name your sprite "coast" as shown below and click OK.

15

8

> pixelpad.io says
>
> Please enter a name for your texture.
>
> coast
>
> OK   Cancel

Notice here how we did **not capitalize** the "c" in coast. This is because we are creating a sprite, not a Class!

Now, you should see a sprite called coast.png below the sprites menu. Notice how it automatically adds .jpg to the end of our coast sprite. The .jpg is the file type.

Note: If you are using a different sprite, it may be .png or something else. Make sure to pay attention to the type. This will be important when we assign it to our Background.

Ok! So, now our game has a coast sprite, but we still haven't assigned it to our Background class. To do this, we will have to write some code inside of our Background class. So, let's head over there!

9 → Click on the 🟦 Background Class, then click on the Start Tab of your editor.

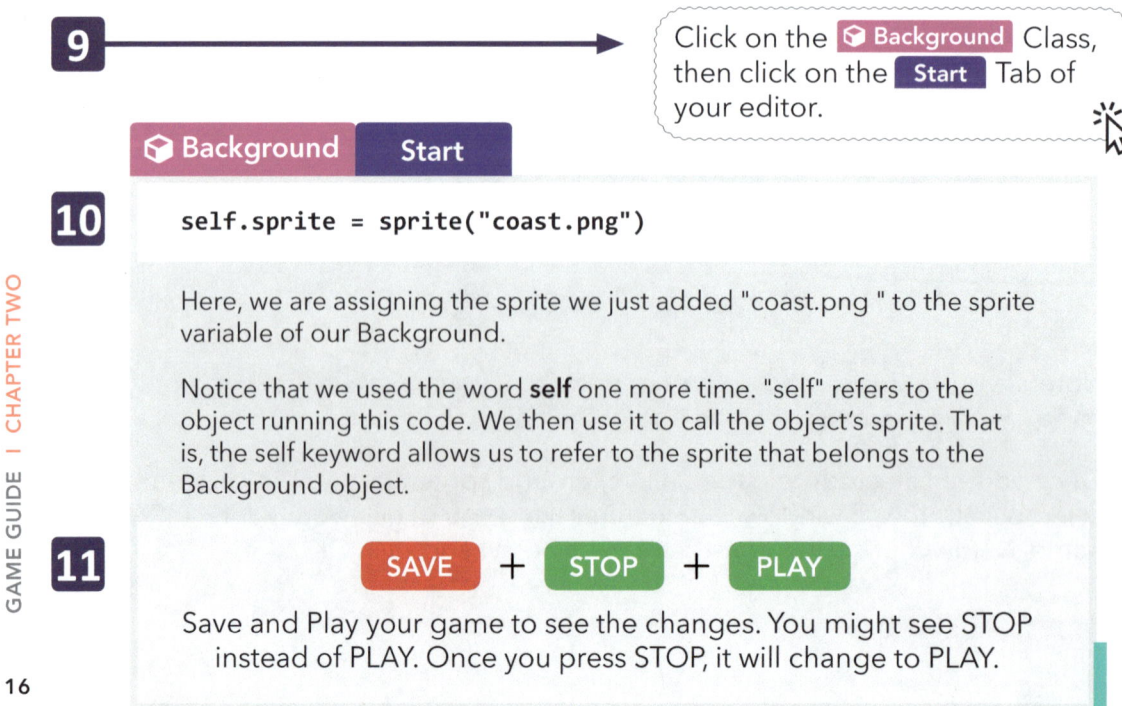

10
```
self.sprite = sprite("coast.png")
```

Here, we are assigning the sprite we just added "coast.png " to the sprite variable of our Background.

Notice that we used the word **self** one more time. "self" refers to the object running this code. We then use it to call the object's sprite. That is, the self keyword allows us to refer to the sprite that belongs to the Background object.

11   SAVE + STOP + PLAY

Save and Play your game to see the changes. You might see STOP instead of PLAY. Once you press STOP, it will change to PLAY.

You should now be able to see your background rendered as the sprite you specified.

Great, we can already see our background in our game! However, the image seems too large and zoomed in. Let's also make this background image a bit smaller by changing its X and Y scale.

Every object has default scaleX and scaleY values set to 1. If we change the scaleX value, we will be changing the width of this object. If we change the scaleY, we will be changing the height of this object. Let's try it out!

12 Click on the Background Class, then click on the Start Tab of your editor.

The **black bolded code** is what you need to add while the grey code is what you have already typed in before. This is to let you know where you need to type the code.

The **X** and **Y** are upper case for **scaleX** and **scaleY**. Make sure to pay attention to **Upper and Lower cases**.

13
```
self.sprite = sprite("coast.png")

self.scaleX = 0.5
self.scaleY = 0.5
```

Here, we're reducing the Background's scale by changing its scaleX and scaleY properties to be 0.5 (This is 50% so half of the original scale).

14   SAVE + PLAY

Save and Play your game to see the changes

17

THE PLAYER

Now that we have our coast background set up, we can add the most important piece of our game: Our player!

The first step is to create our player class.

15

Then, we'll name the new class "Player". Again, notice how we capitalized "P" in Player.

16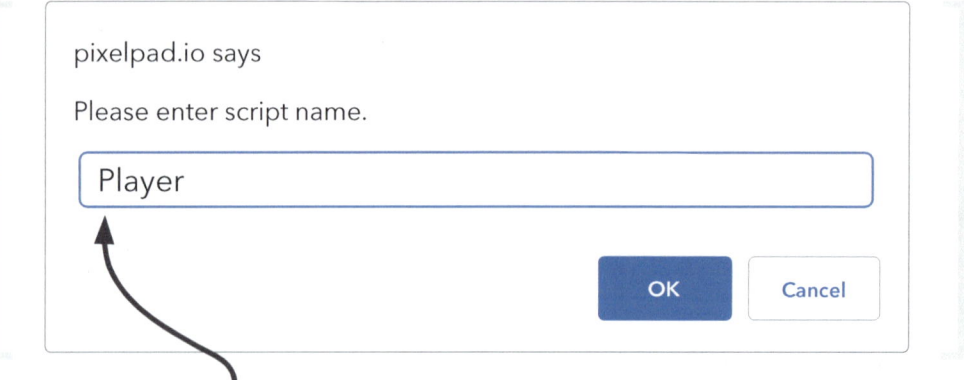

Remember to **capitalize** Class names! In this case, the "P" in Player.

Now, we will add some code that will make the player appear on the screen!

17

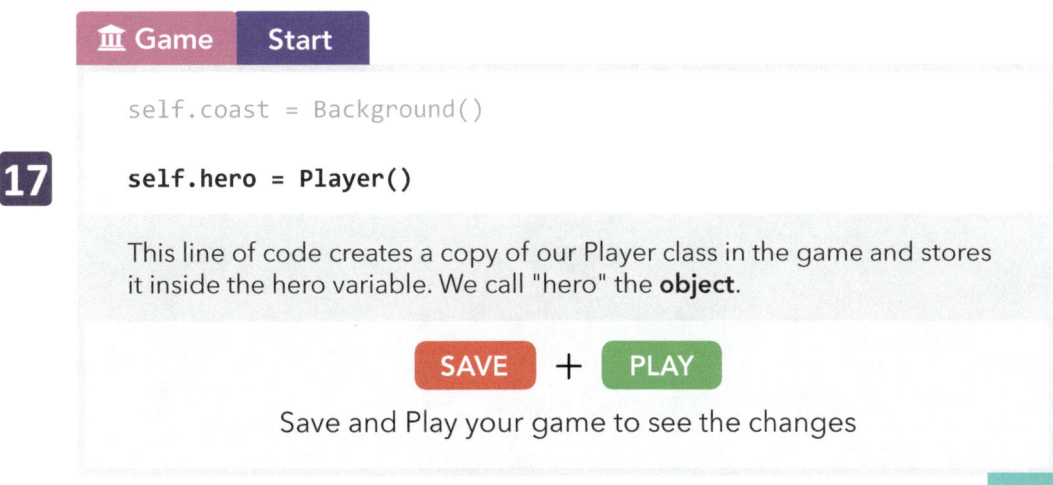

Save and Play your game to see the changes

You may notice that your object shows up, but it says empty image... This is because we haven't assigned our object an image.

Let's add a new sprite by pressing the + icon besides Sprites.

18

For our example, we will be using the Pixelhead Right sprite.

Note: Do not use an animated sprite. We will not cover animation in this book. If you are uploading your own image, make sure the file type is .png and not .jpg to make sure the image background is transparent.

19

Name your sprite "hero" as shown below and click OK.

20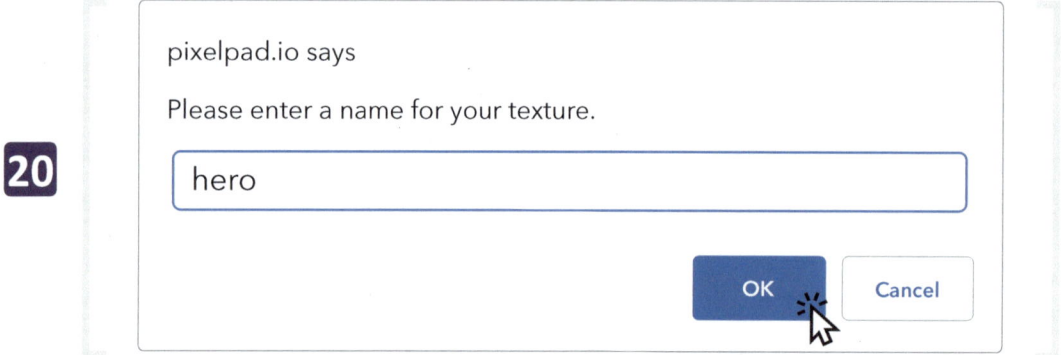

Ok! So, now our game has a hero sprite but we still haven't assigned it to our player. To do this, we will have to write some code inside of our Player class. So, let's head over there!

21 Click on the `Player` Class, then click on the `Start` Tab of your editor.

22 / 23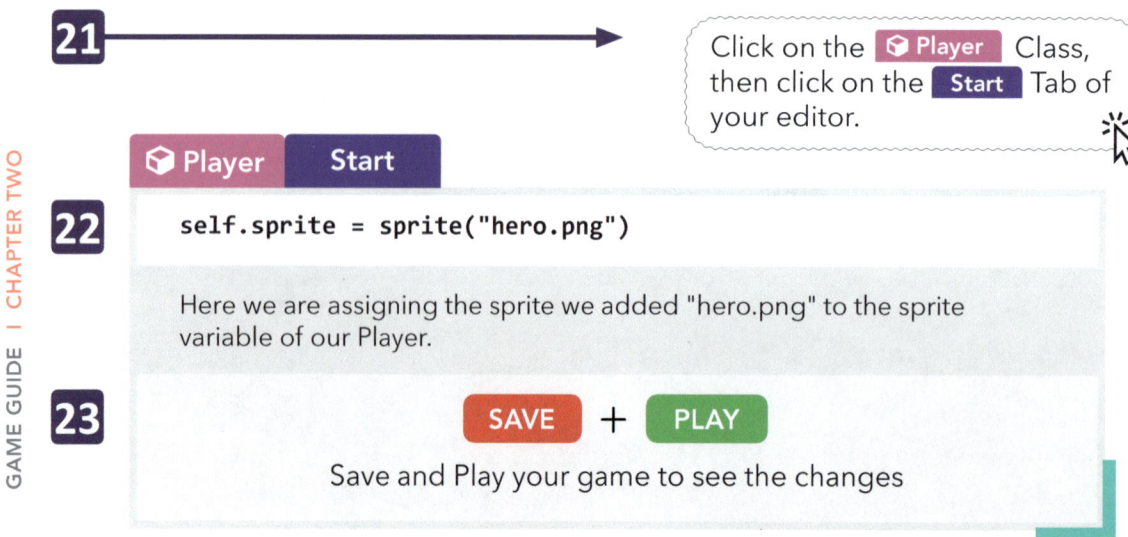

You should now see your player rendered as the sprite you specified in the Player Class.

MOVING THE PLAYER

We're going to manipulate our player's position directly. Simply put, we're going to move our player! For more information on how x and y coordinates work, check out the glossary section on the Cartesian Coordinate System!

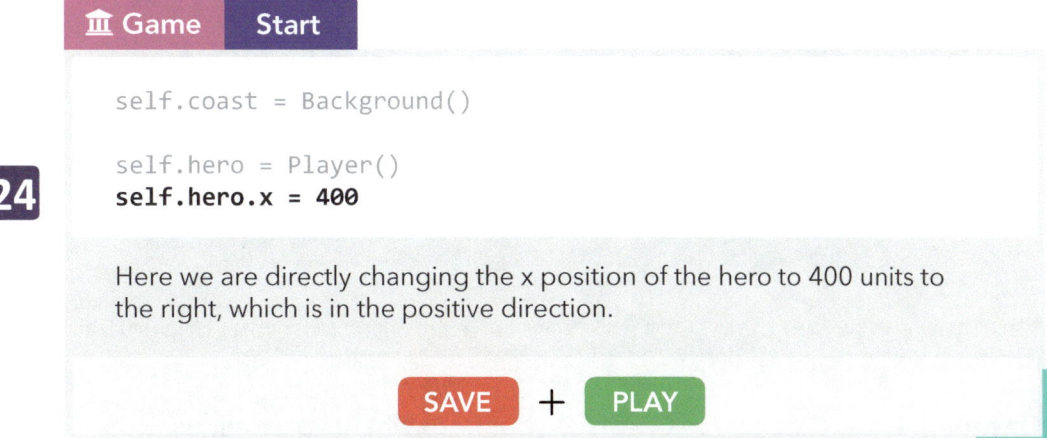

The x-axis moves our player left and right while the y-axis moves it up and down. You can also try changing the y position of your player by using "self.hero.y".

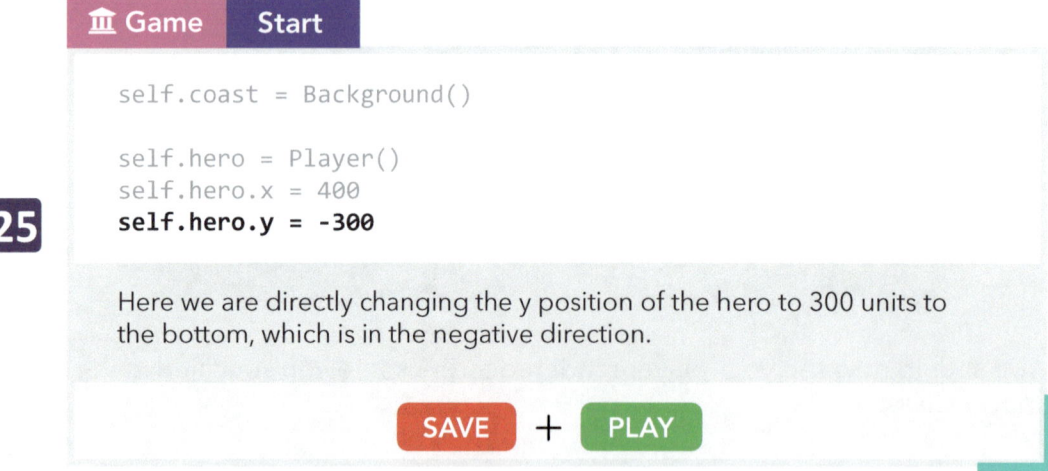

Here we are directly changing the y position of the hero to 300 units to the bottom, which is in the negative direction.

You should now see that your hero moved to different positions depending on the x and y position you gave the object.

Change the x and y positions to place your hero where you want him to start the game.

26

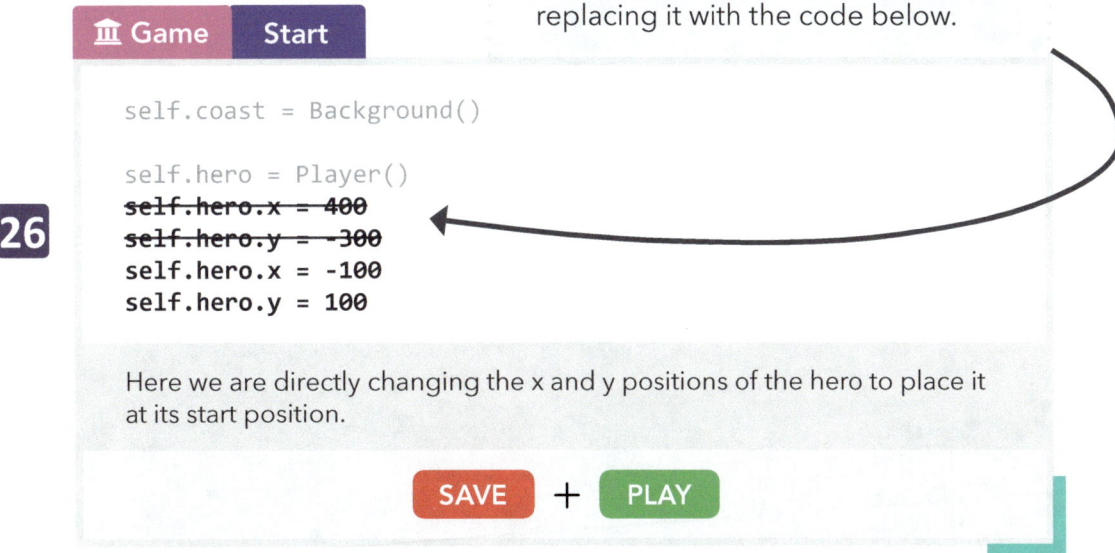

The **crossed out code** means we are **deleting** this code because we are replacing it with the code below.

```
self.coast = Background()

self.hero = Player()
self.hero.x = 400
self.hero.y = -300
self.hero.x = -100
self.hero.y = 100
```

Here we are directly changing the x and y positions of the hero to place it at its start position.

SAVE + PLAY

03.
CHAPTER

THE ENEMY

Our character is pretty cool, but it isn't much of a game if there is nothing in the world besides our player. Let's add some more new objects!

Like the Player, we have to create a Class and add a Sprite from the asset library before coding it inside the Game class.

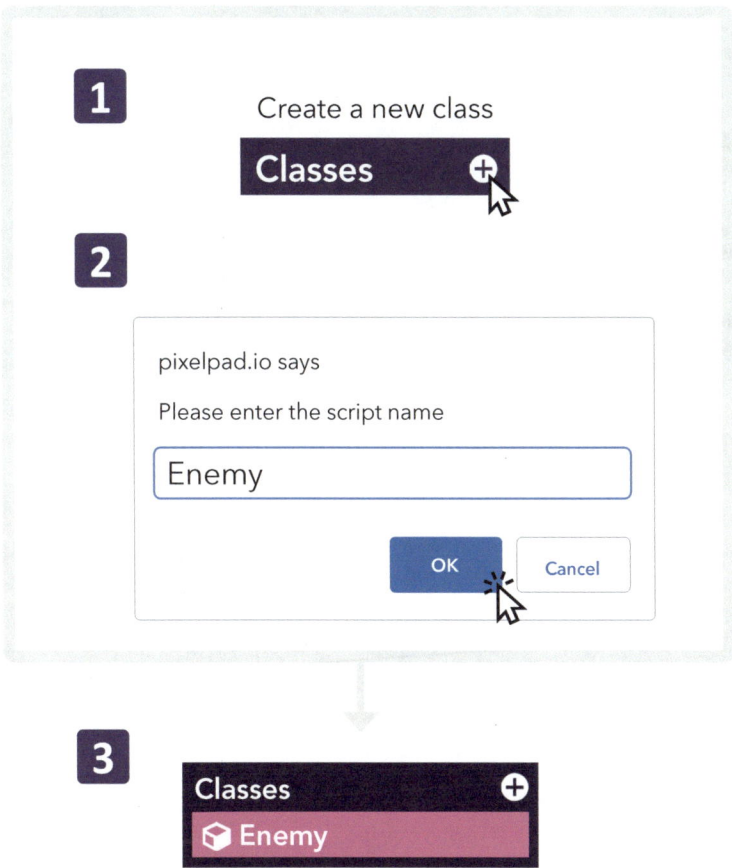

After creating a class we are ready to add it to our game!

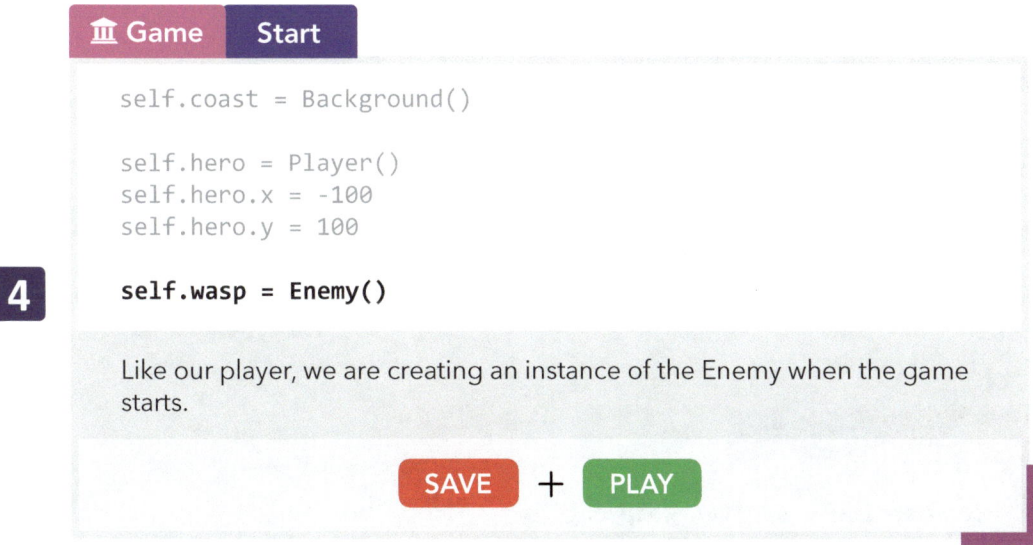

Just like before it's only a blue box. Remember how we fixed that last time? We added a sprite onto the object!

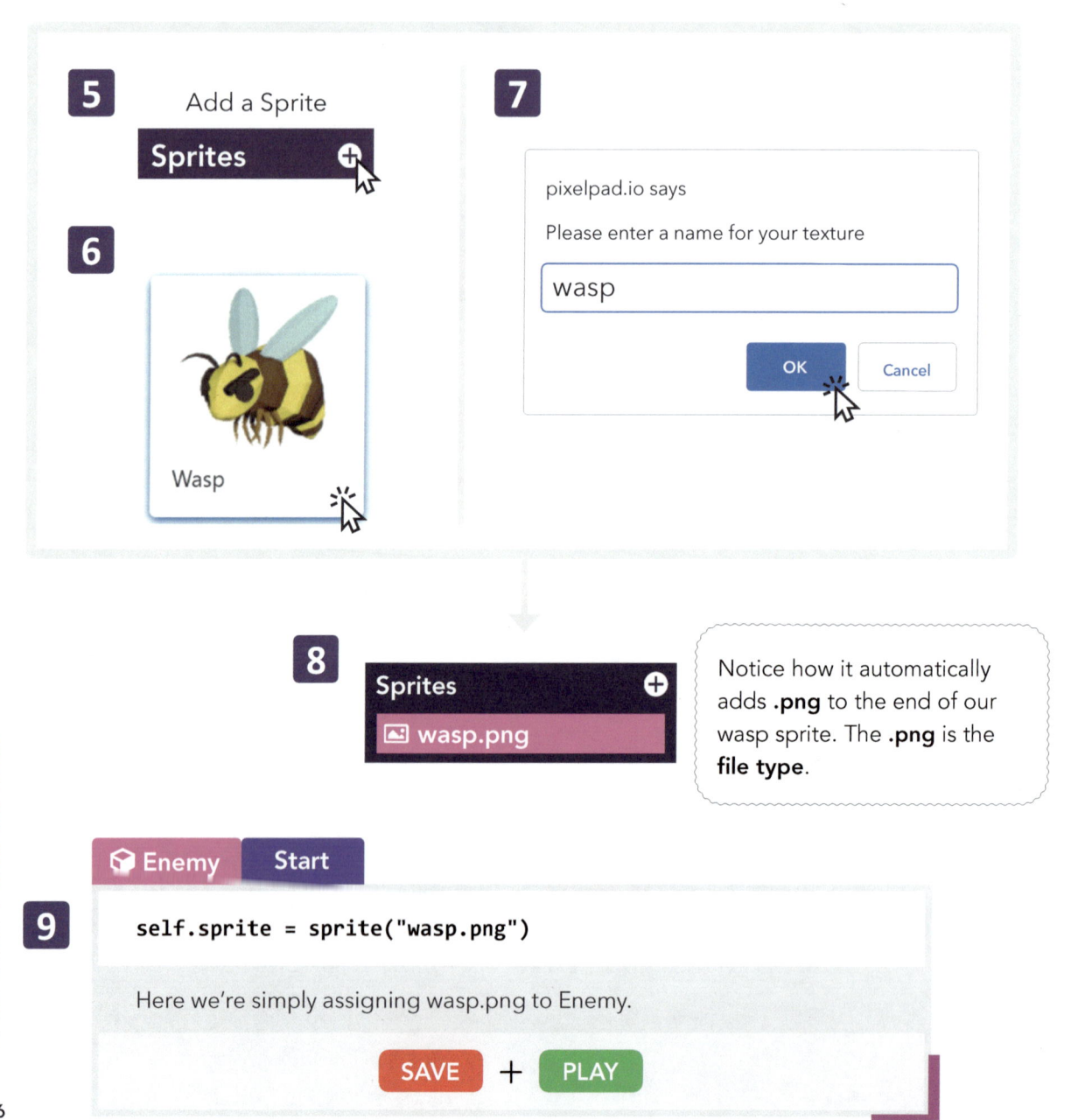

5 Add a Sprite

6

7
pixelpad.io says

Please enter a name for your texture

wasp

OK   Cancel

8 Sprites — wasp.png

Notice how it automatically adds **.png** to the end of our wasp sprite. The **.png** is the **file type**.

Enemy Start

9
```
self.sprite = sprite("wasp.png")
```

Here we're simply assigning wasp.png to Enemy.

SAVE + PLAY

You should now see that our enemy object has a sprite.

You can move it around just like we did with the player by going back to the game class, navigating to the Start Tab, and using the lines:

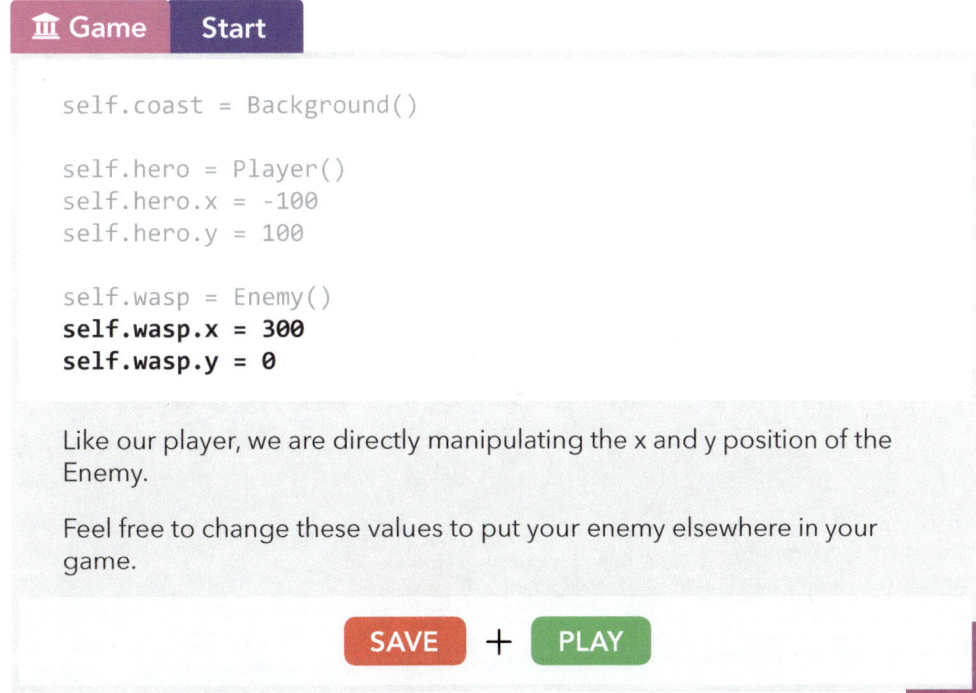

Like our player, we are directly manipulating the x and y position of the Enemy.

Feel free to change these values to put your enemy elsewhere in your game.

We can also use the scale functions we learned before to make our wasp a little smaller to fit better in our game with our player.

Here we're simply reducing the Wasp's size by 70%.

04.
CHAPTER

PLAYER CONTROLS

We now have a bunch of objects placed in our game, but it's not much of a game if we can't interact with it at all.

So, we're going to add movement to the player. To do this, we're going to be adding code to the Loop Tab, which runs again and again so behaviors that we code in the loop tab will happen again and again. For in depth knowledge about Start and Loop, head to "The Game Loop" section in the glossary.

Player | **Loop**

1 `self.x = self.x + 4`

This line refers to the player's current x position, and then sets it to itself + 4.

The result is that the player will look like it is constantly moving to the right.

SAVE + **PLAY**

You will notice that your player keeps moving to the right until it exits your game screen.

This code is saying that whatever the x value was before, it adds 4 to it, and then does that again and again so fast it looks like it is moving smoothly. Kind of like a flipbook animation!

Go ahead and try changing the number!

What happens when it's a higher number? What if it's negative? What if you replace x with y? Test these out, you should be able to get the player to move in any direction.

As fun as it is to watch our player run off in every direction, we want to have control over when it moves and which way it moves. To do that, we are going to need an If Statement.

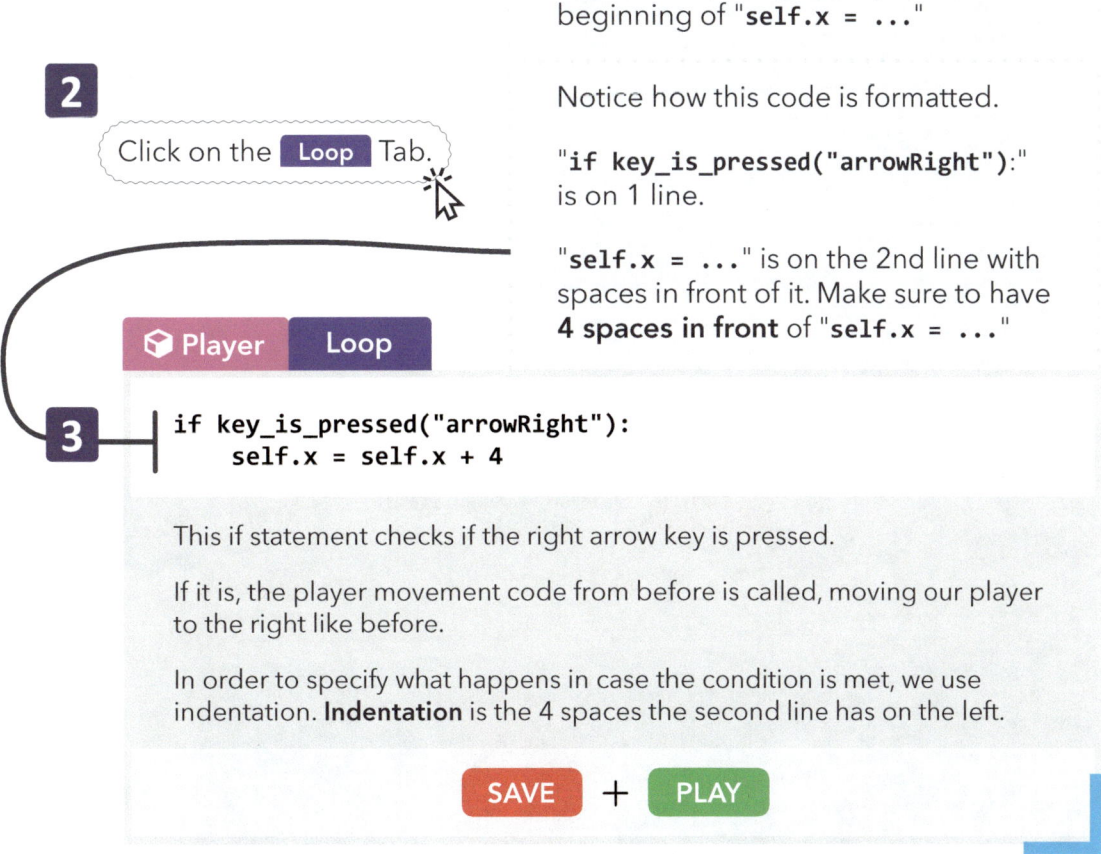

To add more lines at the top, press **Enter/Return** on your keyboard at the beginning of "`self.x = ...`"

2 Click on the Loop Tab.

Notice how this code is formatted.

"`if key_is_pressed("arrowRight"):`" is on 1 line.

"`self.x = ...`" is on the 2nd line with spaces in front of it. Make sure to have **4 spaces in front** of "`self.x = ...`"

3
```
if key_is_pressed("arrowRight"):
    self.x = self.x + 4
```

This if statement checks if the right arrow key is pressed.

If it is, the player movement code from before is called, moving our player to the right like before.

In order to specify what happens in case the condition is met, we use indentation. **Indentation** is the 4 spaces the second line has on the left.

SAVE + PLAY

Now the player should only move when you press down on the right arrow key. Try it out!

Nice, we can already control our player to move right. On new lines underneath, type out similar statements for the left direction.

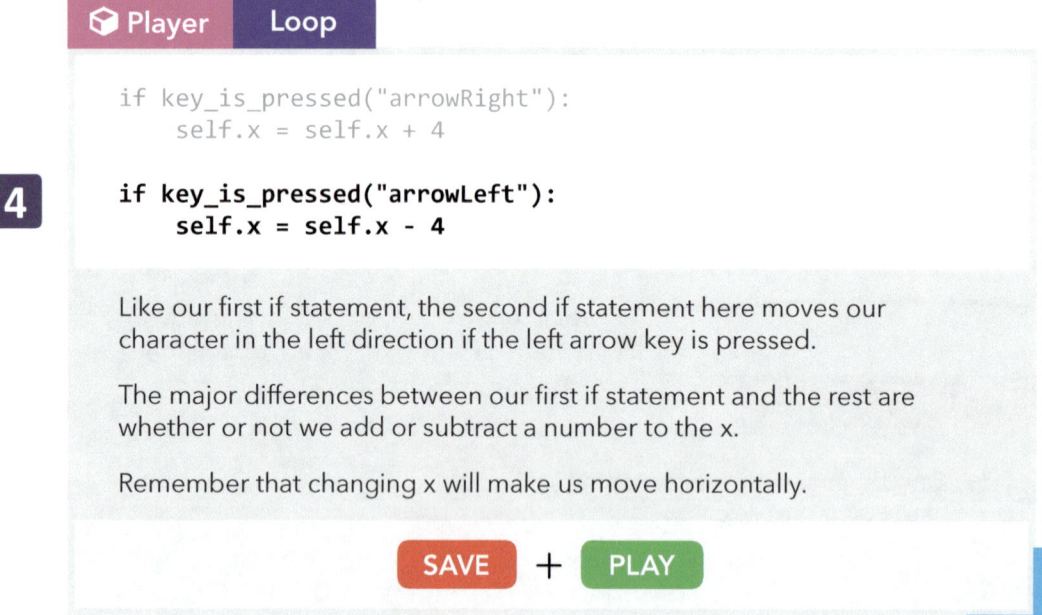

Like our first if statement, the second if statement here moves our character in the left direction if the left arrow key is pressed.

The major differences between our first if statement and the rest are whether or not we add or subtract a number to the x.

Remember that changing x will make us move horizontally.

Your player character should now be able to move left and right using the arrow keys! Test it out and you should be able to move around smoothly.

PLAYER DIRECTIONS

In this section, we will control the direction the player is facing depending on the direction they are moving in. For example, if the player is moving to the right, then they should be facing right.

To do this, we use scaleX to flip the player right and left and we will use if statements to check to see when we should change the direction the player is facing.

Player | **Loop**

5

```
if key_is_pressed("arrowRight"):
    self.x = self.x + 4
    self.scaleX = 1

if key_is_pressed("arrowLeft"):
    self.x = self.x - 4
    self.scaleX = -1
```

Inside the if statements, we check which direction the user wants to go. Then, depending on the key they've pressed, we modify the scaleX property so that the player is facing the direction they are moving in.

When scaleX is 1 (which is its default value), the sprite will face the same direction as when we first assigned it. However, when we change it to -1, the sprite will be "flipped" horizontally in the opposite direction (it will face the opposite direction). Because our hero sprite is initially facing right, when we change scaleX to -1, our sprite will face left. And, when we change it to 1, again, it will face right.

SAVE **PLAY**

Your sprite should now properly change no matter what direction you are moving in!

Great work! If you want to change the movement speed of your player, simply change the number 4 to something else like 0.5 or 2 or 5. Play around with it until it feels right.

It is now time to build our scene, that is, the objects that our player will interact with such as the platforms they can jump on.

To do this, we will need to create a couple more classes and attach sprites to them!

THE PLATFORM

Just like with our background, we'll first need to create a class and then find a sprite from the asset library to attach to it.

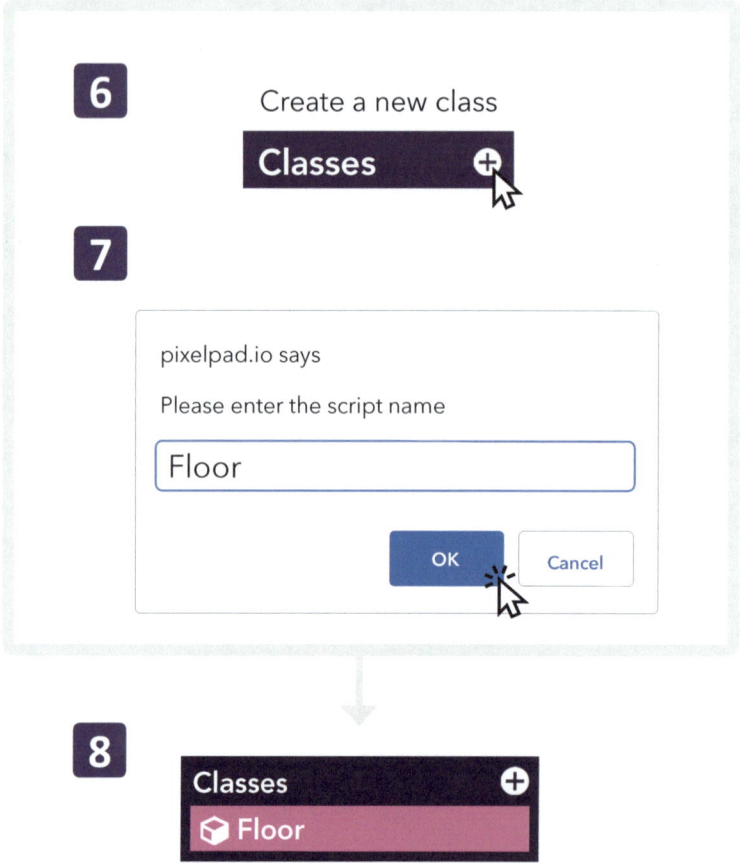

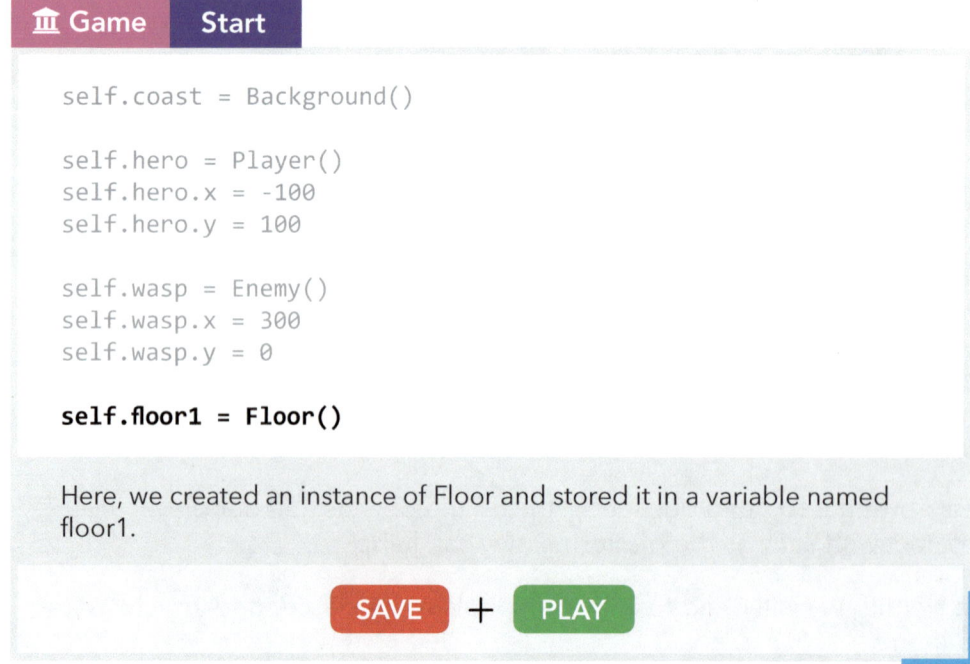

Here, we created an instance of Floor and stored it in a variable named floor1.

Now, let's find a sprite for our floor from the asset library. Remember what happens if we forget this step?

Notice how it automatically adds **.png** to the end of our grassTile sprite. The **.png** is the **file type**.

14 `self.sprite = sprite("grassTile.png")`

Here we are assigning the sprite "grassTile.png" to our Floor sprite variable.

SAVE + **PLAY**

Notice how the tile is not under our player and that 1 tile isn't enough?

Let's first move the tile so that it is somewhere below the player. While we're at it, let's also add another floor object and place it right beside floor1 to make the platform look bigger.

Game | Start

15
```
self.coast = Background()

self.hero = Player()
self.hero.x = -200
self.hero.y = 50

self.wasp = Enemy()
self.wasp.x = 300
self.wasp.y = 0

self.floor1 = Floor()
self.floor1.x = -100
self.floor1.y = -100

self.floor2 = Floor()
self.floor2.x = -200
self.floor2.y = -100
```

Here, we moved our player so it is above the floor tiles we are adding to the game.

Next, we moved floor1 so that it is below the player and we created a second Floor object that we named floor2 and placed it right beside the first one (floor1).

The positions of both floors don't have to match the ones above as long as the floors are next to each other and are somewhere below the player.

SAVE + **PLAY**

37

05. CHAPTER

GRAVITY

Just like in the real world, our player should fall down when they are in the air. This happens because of gravity.

Adding gravity to our game is very simple. We just continuously decrease the player's y coordinate so that they are always moving down toward the bottom of the screen.

Player | **Loop**

```
if key_is_pressed("arrowRight"):
    self.x = self.x + 4
    self.scaleX = 1

if key_is_pressed("arrowLeft"):
    self.x = self.x - 4
    self.scaleX = -1
```

1 `self.y = self.y - 2`

Inside the if statements, we check which direction the user wants to go. Then, depending on the key they've pressed, we modify the scaleX property so that the player is facing the direction they are moving in.

When scaleX is 1 (which is its default value), the sprite will face the same direction as when we first assigned it. However, when we change it to -1, the sprite will be "flipped" horizontally in the opposite direction (it will face the opposite direction). Because our hero sprite is initially facing right, when we change scaleX to -1, our sprite will face left. And, when we change it to 1, again, it will face right.

SAVE + **PLAY**

The player moves down as expected! However, what happens when the player is directly above the platform? It will move down through the platform!

To fix this, we will need to use collisions to figure out when the player has touched the platform.

COLLISIONS

Now we are going to implement collisions between objects.

First of all, what is collision? Think of collision as checking whenever 2 objects touch. When you clap your hands together, they are colliding. When you throw a bouncy ball down, it collides with the ground.

For an in-depth explanation on collisions, head to "Collision" section of the documentation. To get there:

> **Click documentation → PixelPAD2D (Python) → Collision**

To check if 2 things are colliding, we need to use the get_collision() function. We will write code that checks if the player has touched the ground.

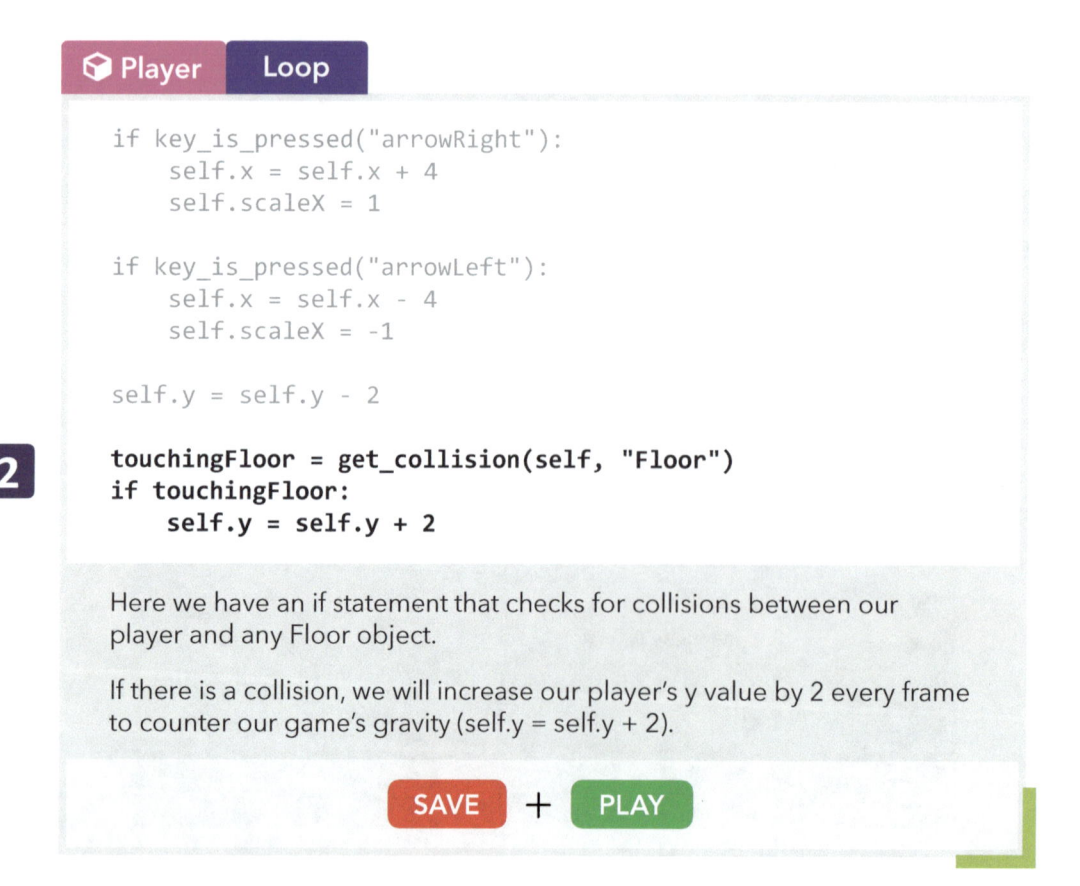

Player | Loop

```python
if key_is_pressed("arrowRight"):
    self.x = self.x + 4
    self.scaleX = 1

if key_is_pressed("arrowLeft"):
    self.x = self.x - 4
    self.scaleX = -1

self.y = self.y - 2

touchingFloor = get_collision(self, "Floor")
if touchingFloor:
    self.y = self.y + 2
```

2

Here we have an if statement that checks for collisions between our player and any Floor object.

If there is a collision, we will increase our player's y value by 2 every frame to counter our game's gravity (self.y = self.y + 2).

SAVE + PLAY

Great! Even though our player keeps falling, once they touch a platform, they stay there. Of course, once they walk off the platform, they will continue to fall again.

Next, we'll look at how to make the player jump!

JUMPING

Now, we will give our player the ability to jump. This is important because to get from one platform to the next, they have to be able to jump. Not only that, the player has to jump and land on top of the enemies to defeat them, just like in Mario!

The player should only be allowed to jump for a limited time before they start to fall down again. Also, we should have control over when they start the jump.

To do that, we need to know if the player is on top of the ground tiles. We will also need a timer to see how long we should increase the player's y value to make them go up.

Okay, now let's create two variables in the Player class.

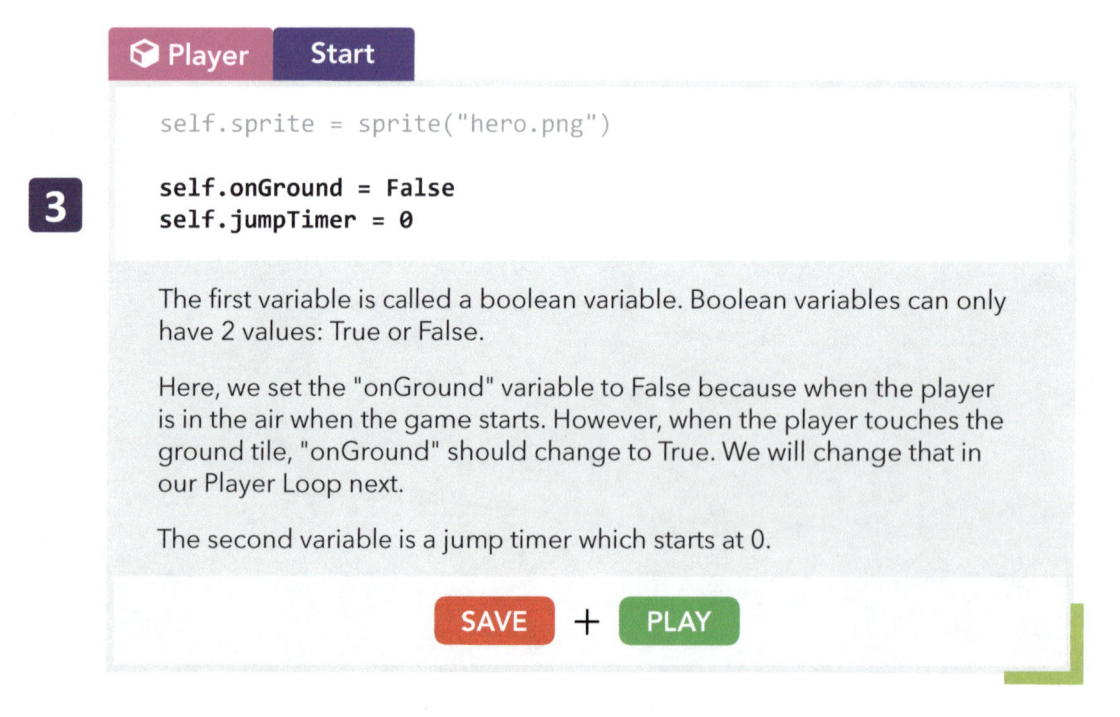

3

Player | **Start**

```
self.sprite = sprite("hero.png")

self.onGround = False
self.jumpTimer = 0
```

The first variable is called a boolean variable. Boolean variables can only have 2 values: True or False.

Here, we set the "onGround" variable to False because when the player is in the air when the game starts. However, when the player touches the ground tile, "onGround" should change to True. We will change that in our Player Loop next.

The second variable is a jump timer which starts at 0.

SAVE + **PLAY**

Now that we have these variables created, let's use them so we can make the player jump!

Notice how this code is formatted. "`self.jumpTimer = 30`" is more spaced, this needs **2 indents** (8 spaces in total).

Note: The "..." is to indicate there is more code below/above, you do NOT need to add the dots.

Player | Loop

4
```
...
touchingFloor = get_collision(self, "Floor")
if touchingFloor:
    self.y = self.y + 2
    self.onGround = True

self.jumpTimer = self.jumpTimer - 1

if key_was_pressed("D"):
    if self.onGround == True:
        self.jumpTimer = 30
        self.onGround = False
```

We changed the value of "onGround" to True when the player collides with a Floor object

Next, we check if the user has pressed the "D" key, which is the key used to make the player jump. Then, inside the first if statement, we check for another condition: This time, if the onGround variable is True (if the player is on the ground).

Because pressing "D" makes the player jump, they should no longer be on the ground, so we have to set the "onGround" variable to False again.

Finally, we set the jump timer to 30 (or any value/duration you want the player to jump for).

Notice the 2 if statements and how one is inside the other. This is called a nested if statement. This means that if the first if statement is not true, then we will never get to the second if statement. For example, in our game, we can only check to see if the player is on the ground when the "D" key is pressed.

Notice that we used key_was_pressed("D") instead of key_is_pressed("D"). The difference is that key_was_pressed() determines whether a keyboard key was pressed down only once.

SAVE + **PLAY**

Oh no, even though we've added quite a bit of code, the player still can't jump!

This is because we haven't actually changed its y value. But before that, remember the jumpTimer variable? Well, we should only really be able to jump when the jump timer is larger than 0. So, let's write an if statement that checks for that first.

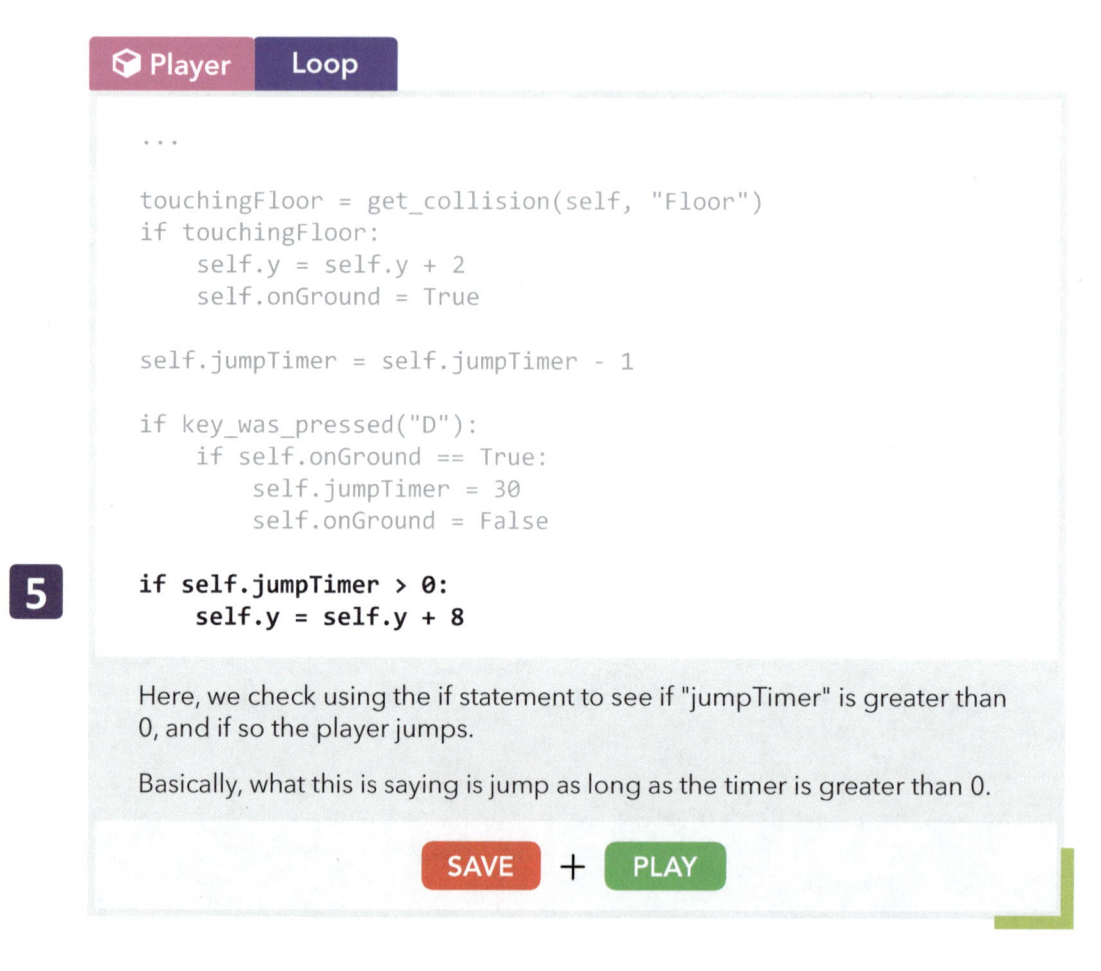

Player | Loop

```
...

touchingFloor = get_collision(self, "Floor")
if touchingFloor:
    self.y = self.y + 2
    self.onGround = True

self.jumpTimer = self.jumpTimer - 1

if key_was_pressed("D"):
    if self.onGround == True:
        self.jumpTimer = 30
        self.onGround = False

if self.jumpTimer > 0:
    self.y = self.y + 8
```

5

Here, we check using the if statement to see if "jumpTimer" is greater than 0, and if so the player jumps.

Basically, what this is saying is jump as long as the timer is greater than 0.

SAVE + **PLAY**

Perfect! Our player can jump now! Feel free to play around with the jumpTimer and the player's y values to make it jump longer and faster.

06.
CHAPTER

ENEMY MOVEMENT

So far, our enemies just sit there without doing anything! To make the game a bit more challenging, let's make them move sideways.

Enemy | **Start**

```
self.sprite = sprite("wasp.png")

self.scaleX = 0.7
self.scaleY = 0.7

self.speed = 1
self.flyRight = True
```

1

We added two new variables in the Enemy class: One that controls the speed of the enemy's movement and the second that keeps track of which direction they're flying.

Next, we'll use these variables along with if statements to make the enemy move in a direction.

Enemy | **Loop**

2

```
if self.flyRight == True:
    self.x += self.speed
    self.scaleX = -0.7

if self.flyRight == False:
    self.x -= self.speed
    self.scaleX = 0.7
```

Here, we check if the Enemy is moving right. If they are, then we'll increase their x value by the value that we assigned to "speed". Similarly, if they are moving left, we'll decrease their x value by the "speed" value.

Just like for our player, we make sure to change the direction of the sprite so that they are facing the correct way when moving.

Notice the += and -=. These are only code shortcuts. For example, self.x += self.speed is a shortcut to self.x = self.x + self.speed and self.x -= self.speed is a shortcut to self.x = self.x - self.speed We also change the scaleX value to flip the enemy to the correct side when moving.

SAVE + **PLAY**

Now our enemy moves to the right. Let's fill up our scene by adding some more enemies!

3

Game | Start

```
...

self.floor2 = Floor()
self.floor2.x = -200
self.floor2.y = -100

self.wasp2 = Enemy()
self.wasp2.x = -300
self.wasp2.y = -200
self.wasp2.speed = 3

self.wasp3 = Enemy()
self.wasp3.x = 300
self.wasp3.y = 100
self.wasp3.speed = 0.5
self.wasp3.flyRight = False
```

We created two new Enemy objects, placed them at different places on the screen, and set their speeds and fly directions differently.

SAVE + **PLAY**

We should have three enemy bees that fly at different speeds and/or directions!

Feel free to play around with the speed and the flyRight of the Enemy objects!

COLLIDING WITH ENEMIES

Similar to what we did when the player hits the floor, we will use the get_collision() function to check if the player has collided with an Enemy object. However, we must also make sure that the enemy can only be destroyed when the player lands on top of it. When the player lands above the enemy, they should also get a jump boost.

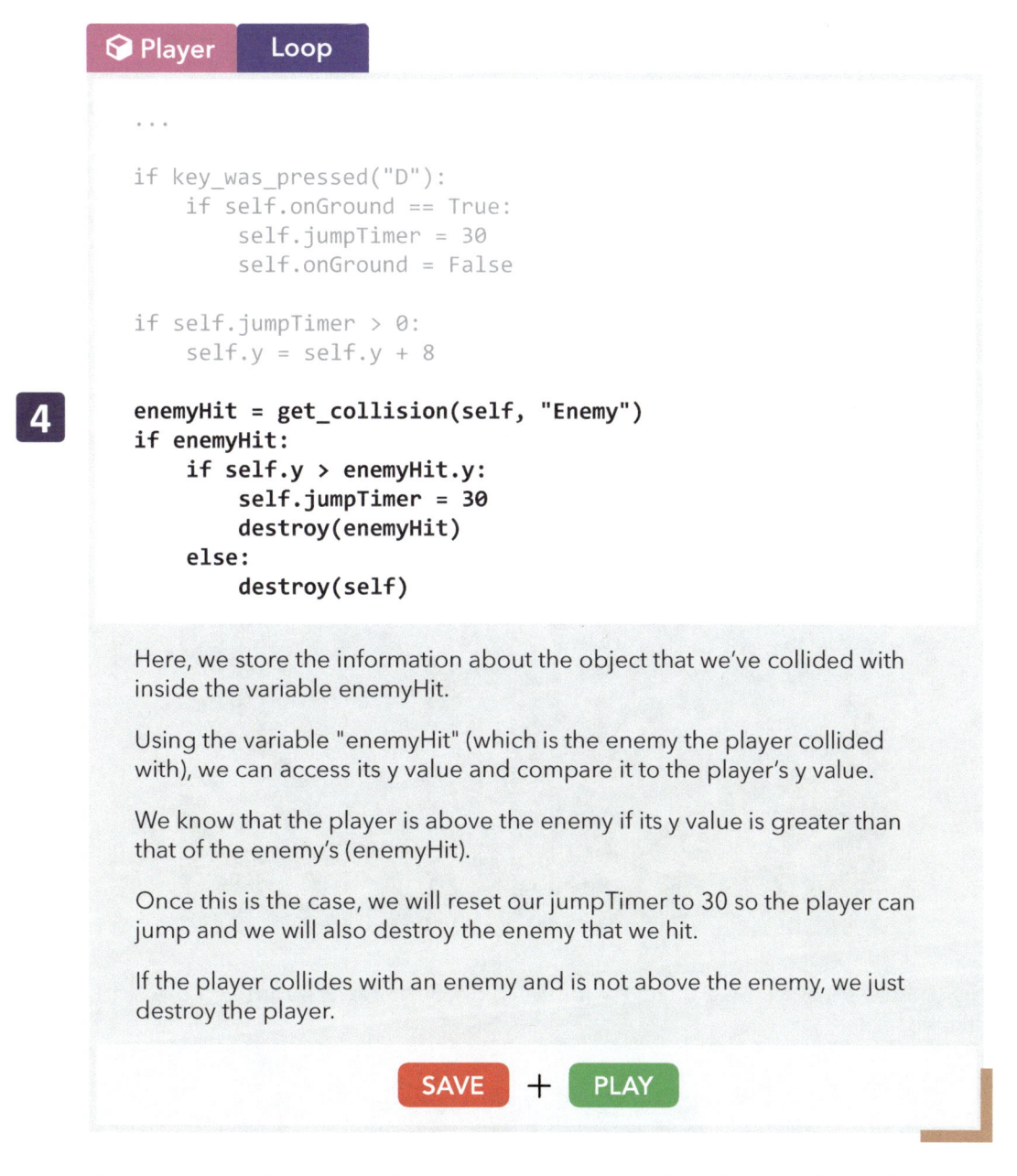

Player | Loop

4

```
...

if key_was_pressed("D"):
    if self.onGround == True:
        self.jumpTimer = 30
        self.onGround = False

if self.jumpTimer > 0:
    self.y = self.y + 8

enemyHit = get_collision(self, "Enemy")
if enemyHit:
    if self.y > enemyHit.y:
        self.jumpTimer = 30
        destroy(enemyHit)
    else:
        destroy(self)
```

Here, we store the information about the object that we've collided with inside the variable enemyHit.

Using the variable "enemyHit" (which is the enemy the player collided with), we can access its y value and compare it to the player's y value.

We know that the player is above the enemy if its y value is greater than that of the enemy's (enemyHit).

Once this is the case, we will reset our jumpTimer to 30 so the player can jump and we will also destroy the enemy that we hit.

If the player collides with an enemy and is not above the enemy, we just destroy the player.

SAVE + **PLAY**

Great! Now we're able to jump and defeat enemies when we land above them. But there is one small problem that we have to fix before we move forward. To see this problem, let's create another floor object and place it close to the player so that they can jump on to it.

Game | **Start**

```
...

self.wasp2 = Enemy()
self.wasp2.x = -300
self.wasp2.y = -200
self.wasp2.speed = 3

self.wasp3 = Enemy()
self.wasp3.x = 300
self.wasp3.y = 100
self.wasp3.speed = 0.5
self.wasp3.flyRight = False
```

5
```
self.floor3 = Floor()
self.floor3.y = 50
```

We created two new enemy objects, placed them at different places on the screen, set their speeds and fly directions differently.

SAVE + **PLAY**

To see the error that we have, try jumping onto the right floor from the side like so,

50

Notice how the player can go inside the floor and not fall when you jump onto it from the side. To fix this small problem, we will make sure that the player is on top of the platform before we land on it. This is actually very similar to what happens when the player lands on top of the enemy.

Player | Loop

6

```
if key_is_pressed("arrowRight"):
    self.x = self.x + 4
    self.scaleX = 1
if key_is_pressed("arrowLeft"):
    self.x = self.x - 4
    self.scaleX = -1

self.y = self.y - 2

touchingFloor = get_collision(self, "Floor")
if touchingFloor:
    if self.y > touchingFloor.y + 50:
        self.y = self.y + 2
        self.onGround = True

self.jumpTimer = self.jumpTimer - 1

...
```

Here, we added code inside the if statement that checks to see if the player's y value is greater than the y value of the floor object that they've collided with. Again, this will make sure that the player is above the floor.

Notice also how we added 50 to the floor object's y value. This is because an object's y value is actually at the center of its vertical height. So, when the player jumps, their y may be larger than the floor's y value even if only a portion of the player is above the floor. Adding 50 makeups for this difference.

SAVE + **PLAY**

07. CHAPTER

SHOOTING PROJECTILE

Beside jumping on top of enemies to destroy them, our player will also be able to shoot projectiles at them.

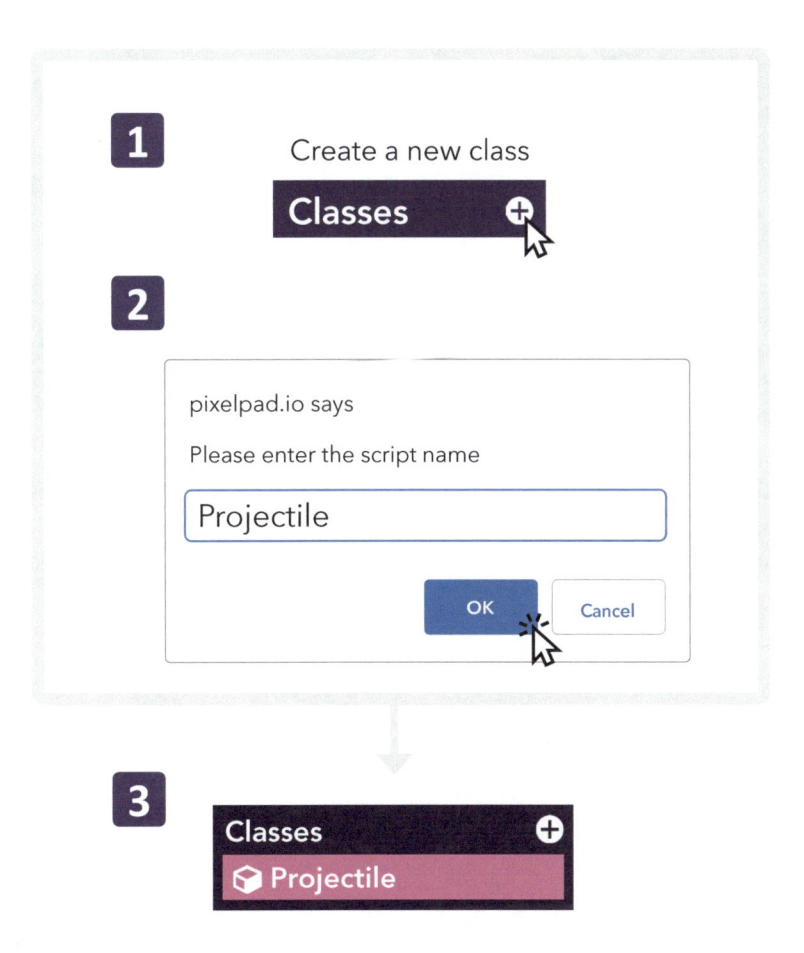

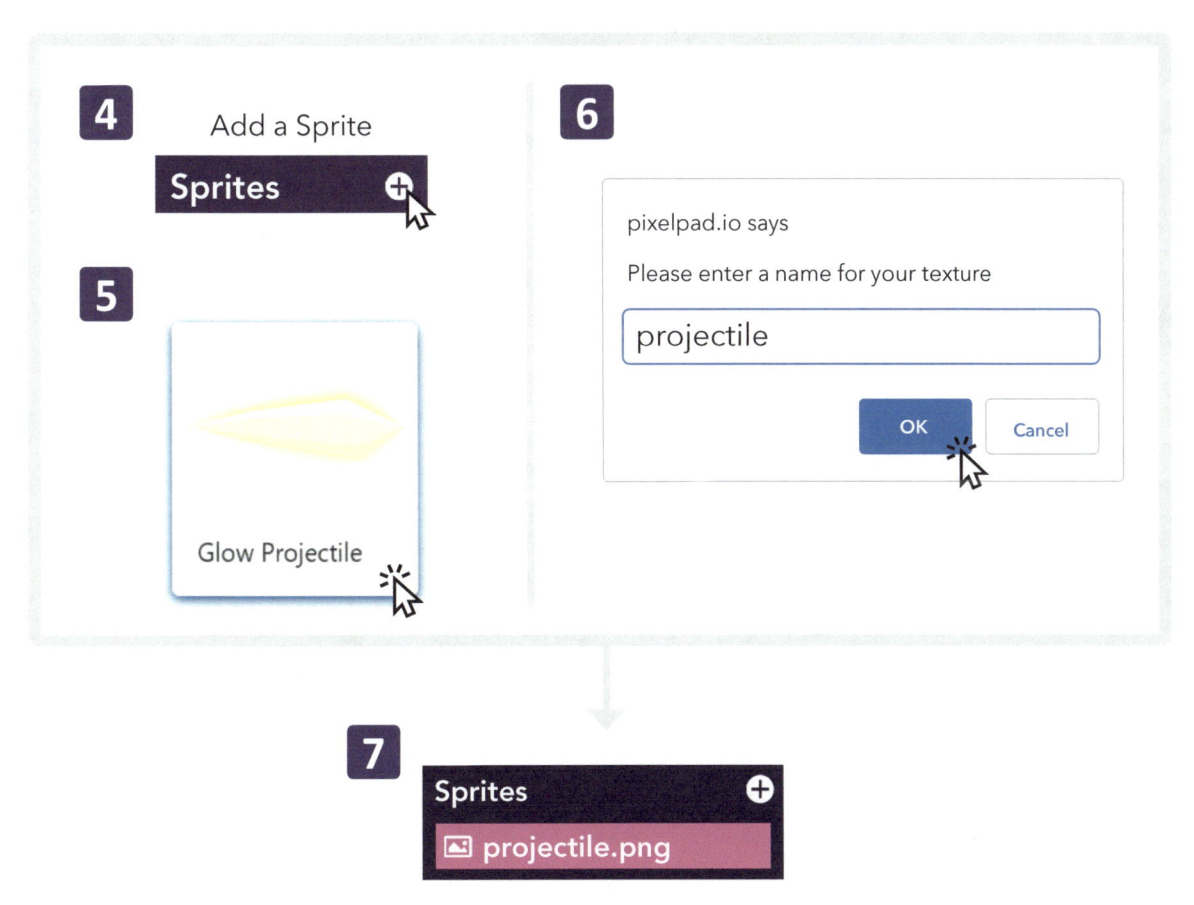

1 Create a new class

Classes ⊕

2

pixelpad.io says

Please enter the script name

Projectile

OK   Cancel

3

Classes ⊕
🎁 Projectile

4 Add a Sprite

Sprites ⊕

5

Glow Projectile

6

pixelpad.io says

Please enter a name for your texture

projectile

OK   Cancel

7

Sprites ⊕
🖼 projectile.png

8

Projectile | Start

```
self.sprite = sprite("projectile.png")

self.scaleX = 0.7
self.scaleY = 0.7
```

Here, we've assigned the "projectile.png" sprite to our projectile object. Then, we reduce the object's scale by modifying scaleX and scaleY.

We will also give our projectile a speed and a direction.

9

Projectile | Start

```
self.sprite = sprite("projectile.png")

self.scaleX = 0.7
self.scaleY = 0.7

self.speed = 5
self.movingRight = True
```

Here, we've added the variable "movingRight" to see if the projectile is moving left or right and the variable speed to control the speed at which the projectile travels.

Next, we'll add a couple of if statements inside the Projectile Loop tab to control when the projectile moves.

10

Projectile | Loop

```
if self.movingRight == True:
    self.x += self.speed
    self.scaleX = 0.7

if self.movingRight == False:
    self.x -= self.speed
    self.scaleX = -0.7
```

We've written two if statements that check which direction the projectile is moving:

In the first if statement, we check if the projectile is moving in the right direction. If it is, then we will increase its x value by the speed variable that we created in the start tab just earlier.

In the second if statement, we check if it's moving in the left direction and if so, we decrease its y value by the speed.

We are also changing the scaleX variable to flip the projectile to the right direction when moving.

Okay, now we will give the player the ability to shoot the projectile when the user presses a key. So, as you might have guessed, we'll have to write some code inside the player class.

Player | **Loop**

```
if key_is_pressed("arrowRight"):
    self.x = self.x + 4
    self.scaleX = 1
    self.facingRight = True
if key_is_pressed("arrowLeft"):
    self.x = self.x - 4
    self.scaleX = -1
    self.facingRight = False

self.y = self.y - 2

touchingFloor = get_collision(self, "Floor")
if touchingFloor:
    if self.y > touchingFloor.y + 50:
        self.y = self.y + 2
        self.onGround = True

self.jumpTimer = self.jumpTimer - 1
```

11
```
if key_was_pressed("F"):
    newProjectile = Projectile()
    newProjectile.x = self.x
    newProjectile.y = self.y
```

```
if key_was_pressed("D"):
    if self.onGround == True:
        self.jumpTimer = 30
        self.onGround = False

...
```

Here, we write an if statement that checks if the user has pressed the F key. When they do, we create a new projectile object and set both its x and y values to the player's x and y values respectively.

We are also changing the scaleX variable to flip the projectile to the right direction when moving.

SAVE + **PLAY**

Great! We can now shoot projectile objects when we press the F key.

However, you might have noticed something that needs to be fixed. When our player is facing left, the projectile beams still move to the right. Also, the projectiles seem too big for our player.

Let's head to our Player class to make the first change.

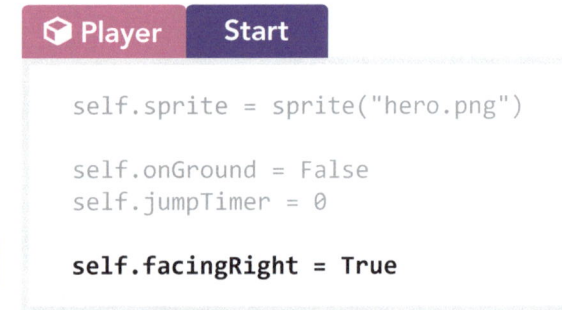

Player | Start

```
self.sprite = sprite("hero.png")

self.onGround = False
self.jumpTimer = 0
```

12

```
self.facingRight = True
```

Here, we've added a boolean variable that keeps track of which direction the player is facing.

Player | **Loop**

13

```
if key_is_pressed("arrowRight"):
    self.x = self.x + 4
    self.scaleX = 1
    self.facingRight = True
if key_is_pressed("arrowLeft"):
    self.x = self.x - 4
    self.scaleX = -1
    self.facingRight = False

self.y = self.y - 2

touchingFloor = get_collision(self, "Floor")
if touchingFloor:
    if self.y > touchingFloor.y + 50:
        self.y = self.y + 2
        self.onGround = True

self.jumpTimer = self.jumpTimer - 1

if key_was_pressed("F"):
    newProjectile = Projectile()
    newProjectile.x = self.x
    newProjectile.y = self.y
    newProjectile.movingRight = self.facingRight

if key_was_pressed("D"):
    if self.onGround == True:
        self.jumpTimer = 30
        self.onGround = False

...
```

First, we updated our if statements so that every time our player is facing a new direction, we update our facingRight variable that we added earlier.

Lastly, since the facingRight variable has the information about which direction the player is facing, we use it to also update the movingRight variable that we created in the newProjectile class.

SAVE + **PLAY**

Great! Our player can now shoot projectiles that are rotated and move in the direction the player is facing!

Let's now make our projectiles effective, making them destroy an enemy once they touch each other. Also, so far, our Enemy isn't able to destroy the player once they touch it.

So, we'll have to make the enemy be able to destroy the player once and enemy collide in such a way that the player is not above the enemy.

Let's start by making both the projectile and enemy disappear when they collide!

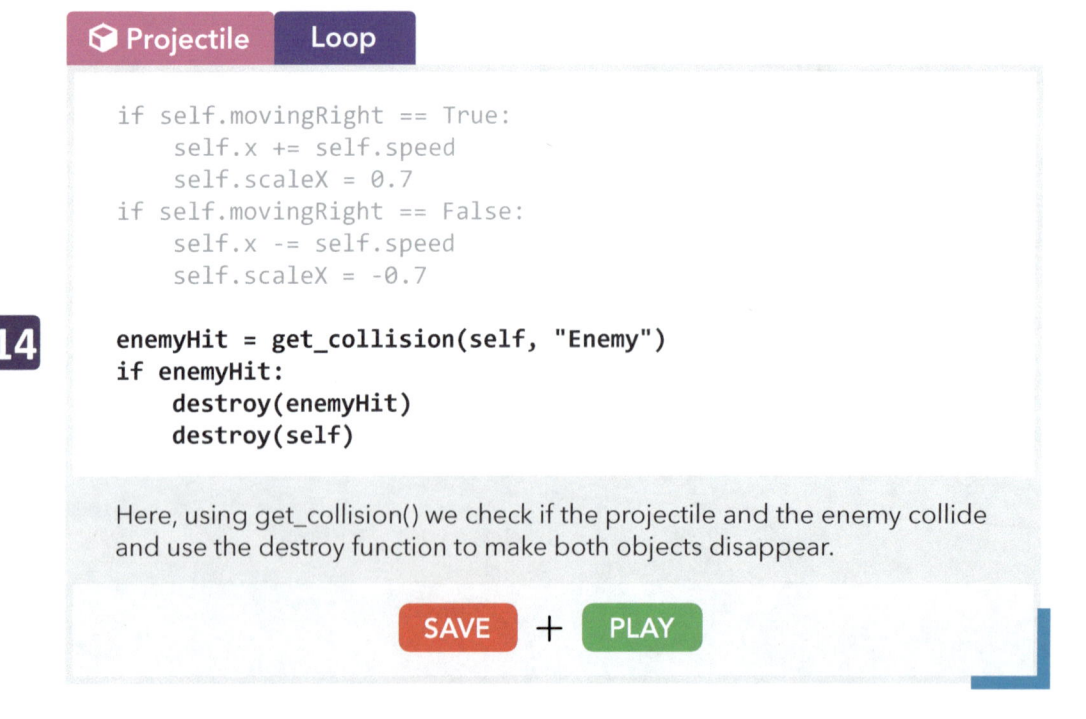

Projectile | **Loop**

```
if self.movingRight == True:
    self.x += self.speed
    self.scaleX = 0.7
if self.movingRight == False:
    self.x -= self.speed
    self.scaleX = -0.7

enemyHit = get_collision(self, "Enemy")
if enemyHit:
    destroy(enemyHit)
    destroy(self)
```

14

Here, using get_collision() we check if the projectile and the enemy collide and use the destroy function to make both objects disappear.

SAVE + **PLAY**

Great! Now, both our projectile and enemy disappear when they collide!

GAME GUIDE | CHAPTER SEVEN

58

08.
CHAPTER

ROOMS

Next, we'll be exploring our world beyond one single screen by adding different rooms to explore!

We'll also learn how to create doors or portals between rooms, and how to tell the game where each one takes you using variables.

Let's get started by creating a room!

The first step to create our **Room** is to click on the white plus icon ⊕ next to the Rooms menu.

1   Rooms ⊕

A pop-up will appear to name it, just like creating a new class and sprite. Call this one "Level1" and then press OK.

2

pixelpad.io says

Please enter room name.

Level1

OK   Cancel

Notice how we now have Level1 under Rooms.

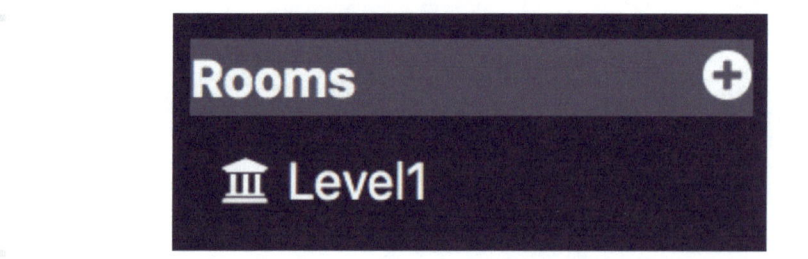

3

Rooms ⊕
🏛 Level1

Up to this point we've just been adding things to our Game Class, but now that we are getting the ability to switch between rooms, we need to keep all of our objects organized in their individual rooms.

To do this, we need to:

4

Open the 🏛 **Game** Class and go to the **Start** tab.

Highlight all the code with your mouse, and copy it with Ctrl+C

5

🏛 **Game** | **Start**

```
self.coast = Background()

self.hero = Player()
self.hero.x = -200
self.hero.y = 50

self.wasp = Enemy()
self.wasp.x = 300
self.wasp.y = 0

self.floor1 = Floor()
self.floor1.x = -100
self.floor1.y = -100

self.floor2 = Floor()
self.floor2.x = -200
self.floor2.y = -100

self.wasp2 = Enemy()
self.wasp2.x = -300
self.wasp2.y = -200
self.wasp2.speed = 3

self.wasp3 = Enemy()
self.wasp3.x = 300
self.wasp3.y = 100
self.wasp3.speed = 0.5
self.wasp3.flyRight = False

self.floor3 = Floor()
self.floor3.y = 50
```

Hold "CTRL" then press "C" to copy

We are highlighting everything in Game Start.

Here is what we have so far as an example. Your Level1 may look different depending on what you've added!

6 Open the 🏛 **Level1** Class and go to the **Start** tab.

Paste your code that you copied back in the Game class with Ctrl+V

7

🏛 **Level1** **Start**

```
self.coast = Background()

self.hero = Player()
self.hero.x = -200
self.hero.y = 50

self.wasp = Enemy()
self.wasp.x = 300
self.wasp.y = 0

self.floor1 = Floor()
self.floor1.x = -100
self.floor1.y = -100

self.floor2 = Floor()
self.floor2.x = -200
self.floor2.y = -100

self.wasp2 = Enemy()
self.wasp2.x = -300
self.wasp2.y = -200
self.wasp2.speed = 3

self.wasp3 = Enemy()
self.wasp3.x = 300
self.wasp3.y = 100
self.wasp3.speed = 0.5
self.wasp3.flyRight = False

self.floor3 = Floor()
self.floor3.y = 50
```

All this code was originally in the Game Class.

Once you've got the code safely in your Level1 class,

8 **Delete the code from Game class. We only want one copy of it!**

SAVE + PLAY

It will look like everything is gone! Don't worry. We just need to tell the Game class which room we want to start in.

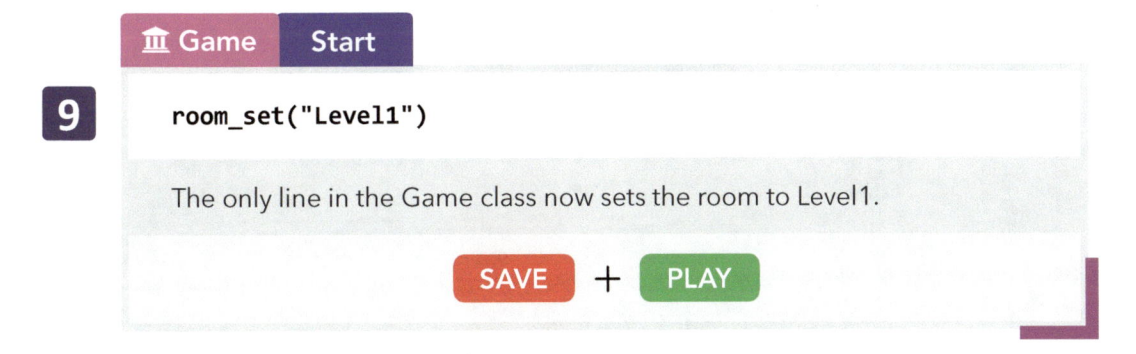

9

🏛 Game | Start

```
room_set("Level1")
```

The only line in the Game class now sets the room to Level1.

SAVE + PLAY

At this point it should all be back to the way it was before. The only difference is now we can add new rooms and switch between them!

PORTALS

To switch between rooms, the first step is to create a new class and attach a sprite to it. Then, when the player collides with it, they'll be taken to a new room.

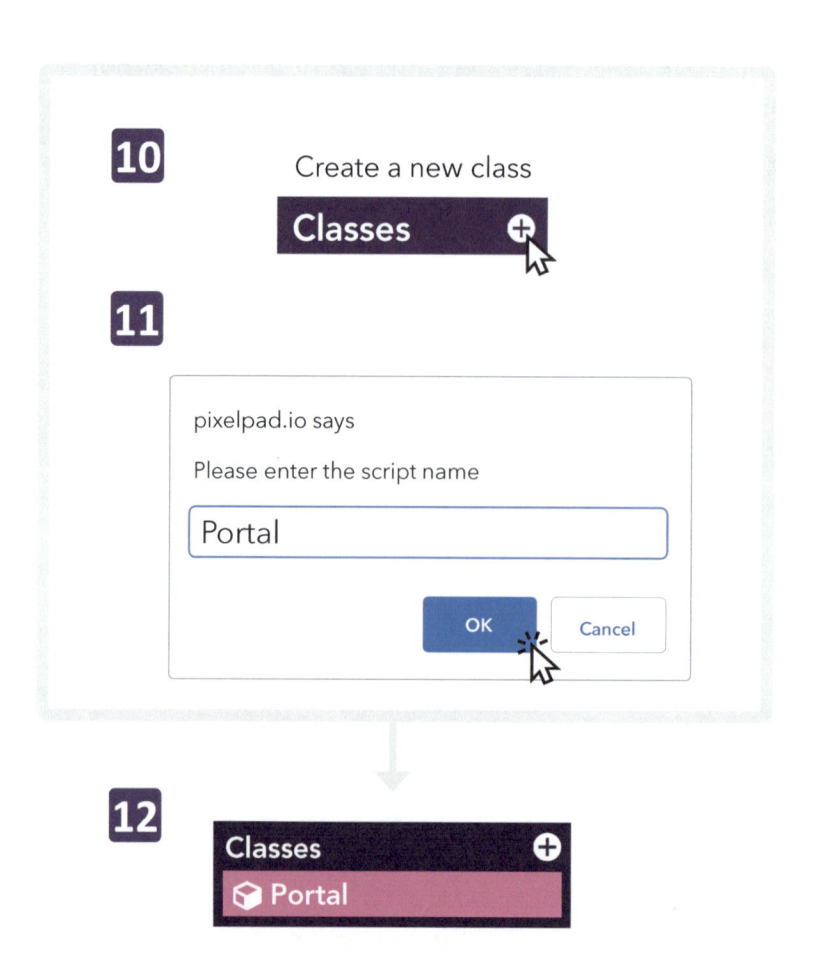

13 Add a Sprite

Sprites ⊕

14 Spaceship Checkpoint

15

pixelpad.io says

Please enter a name for your texture

portal

OK   Cancel

16

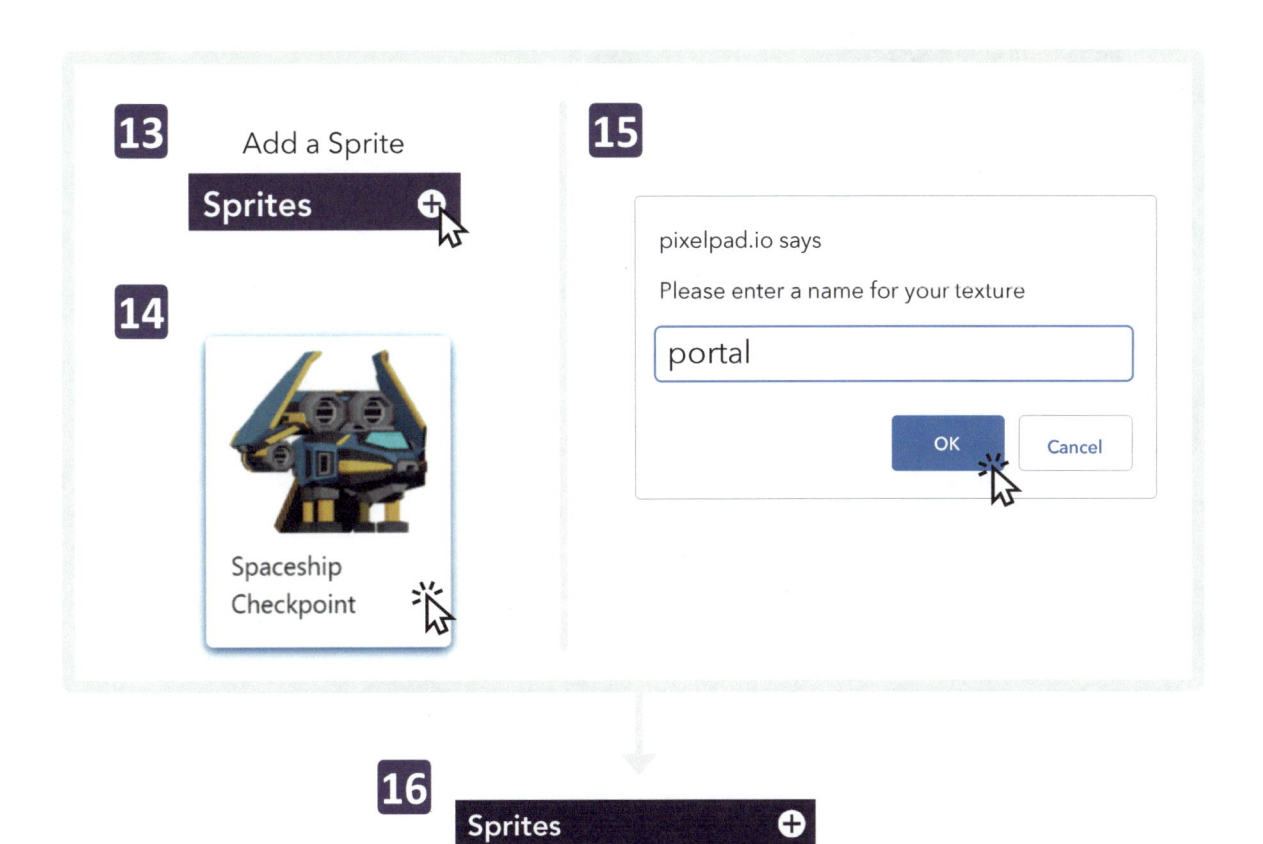

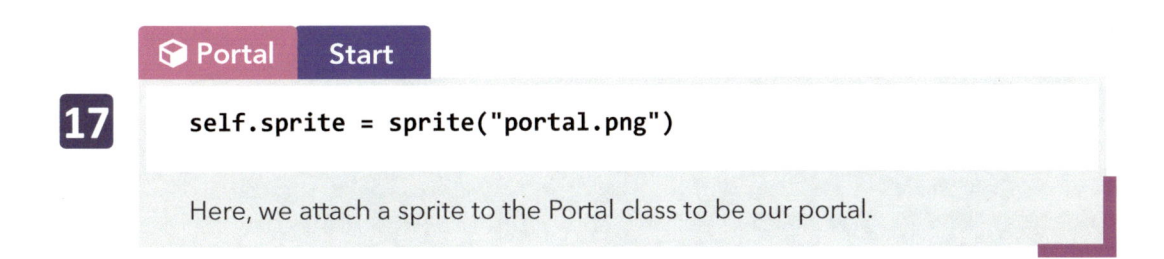

Sprites ⊕

🖼 portal.png

Portal | Start

17
```
self.sprite = sprite("portal.png")
```

Here, we attach a sprite to the Portal class to be our portal.

🏛 Level1 | Start

```
...

self.floor2 = Floor()
self.floor2.x = -200
self.floor2.y = -100

self.floor3 = Floor()
self.floor3.y = 50
```

18
```
self.ship = Portal()
self.ship.x = 350
self.ship.y = 220

self.floor4 = Floor()
self.floor4.x = 300
self.floor4.y = 100

self.floor5 = Floor()
self.floor5.x = 400
self.floor5.y = 100
```

Here we simply create the portal object in our room and place it somewhere in the top right corner of the screen.

We also create two new floor objects so our ship can stand on them.

SAVE + **PLAY**

While we're at it, let's also create a second room that has a player, a portal and some platform to walk on.

19 Create a new Room

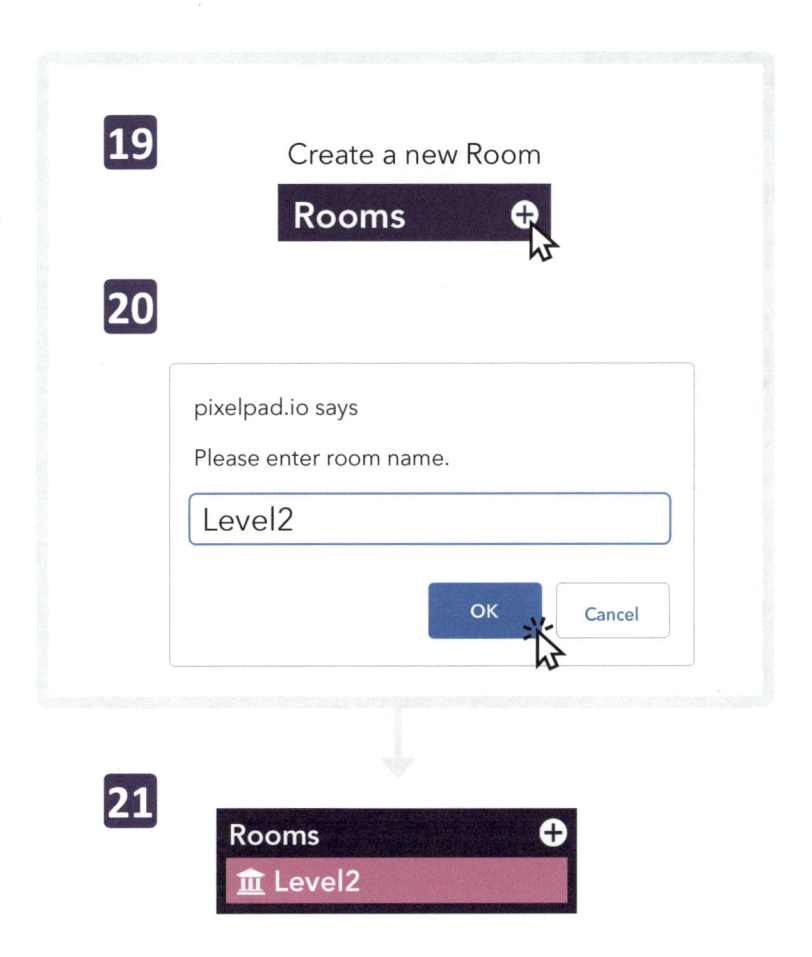

20 pixelpad.io says

Please enter room name.

Level2

OK   Cancel

21 Rooms

Level2

Now let's go to the Level2 Room and create a new room filled with new enemies and platforms!

🏛 Level2 — Start

22

```
self.coast = Background()

self.hero = Player()
self.hero.x = -400
self.hero.y = 200

self.floor1 = Floor()
self.floor1.x = -400
self.floor1.y = -200

self.floor2 = Floor()
self.floor2.x = -305
self.floor2.y = -200

self.floor3 = Floor()

self.floor4 = Floor()
self.floor4.x = -95

self.floor5 = Floor()
self.floor5.x = 500
self.floor5.y = -200

self.wasp1 = Enemy()
self.wasp1.speed = 3
self.wasp1.y = 200

self.wasp2 = Enemy()
self.wasp2.speed = 1

self.wasp3 = Enemy()
self.wasp3.flyRight = False
self.wasp3.y = -150

self.wasp4 = Enemy()
self.wasp4.flyRight = False
self.wasp4.y = 150

self.ship = Portal()
self.ship.x = 350
self.ship.y = 20

self.floor6 = Floor()
self.floor6.x = 300
self.floor6.y = -100

self.floor7 = Floor()
self.floor7.x = 400
self.floor7.y = -100
```

Here we create the Portal object in level 2 as well as the player, the background and a few floor objects so that the player will not just fall down below the screen when they reach level2.

Also, notice how we've placed our objects in different places on the screen. This is because we don't want the 2 levels that we've created so far to look identical.

Feel free to position your objects anywhere you like as you construct your second level. For example, you can create more enemies and have them move faster. And/or place the portal somewhere that is hard to get to.

SAVE + PLAY

Great! This is how our level 2 scene looks so far. Again, feel free to make it look different!

Next, we're going to determine what happens when the portal and the player collide using the function get_collision()

Portal | Loop

23

```
portalHit = get_collision(self, "Player")
if portalHit:
    room_set("Level2")
```

Here we check if the portal has collided with the player, and if it does, we set the room to level 2.

SAVE + PLAY

If you tried walking into the portal in Level2, you'll notice that you're always going back to Level2. That's because if we check out our code, it is always telling us to go back to Level2.

To fix this, we'll need to give each portal a unique destination. We'll create a new variable called "destination".

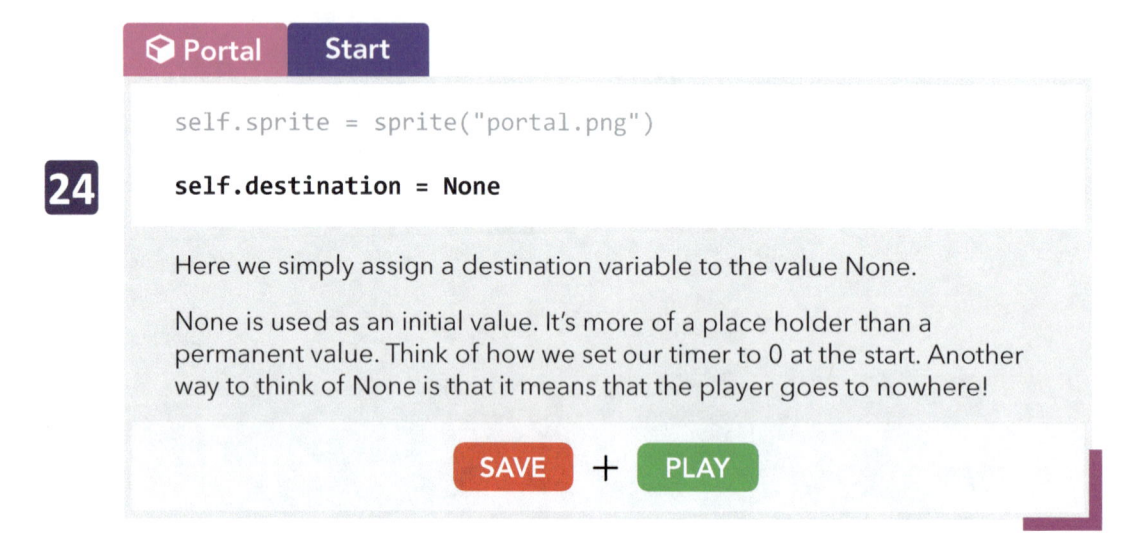

24

Portal — Start

```
self.sprite = sprite("portal.png")
self.destination = None
```

Here we simply assign a destination variable to the value None.

None is used as an initial value. It's more of a place holder than a permanent value. Think of how we set our timer to 0 at the start. Another way to think of None is that it means that the player goes to nowhere!

SAVE + PLAY

Now when we collide with the portal, we check where the destination leads us. None means it goes nowhere! Later, we can change destination to Level1.

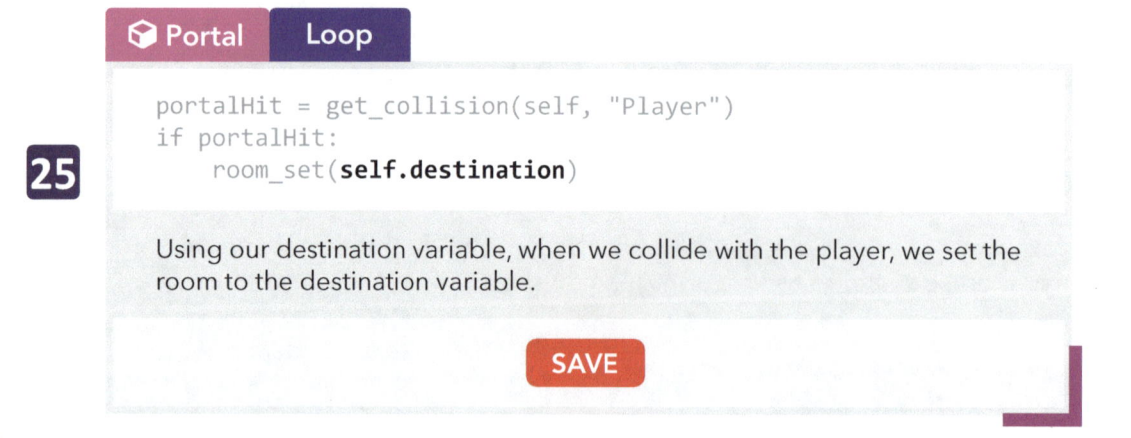

25

Portal — Loop

```
portalHit = get_collision(self, "Player")
if portalHit:
    room_set(self.destination)
```

Using our destination variable, when we collide with the player, we set the room to the destination variable.

SAVE

We'll need to change the destination variable when we create the portal before we can play.

🏛 Level1 — Start

26
```
...

self.ship = Portal()
self.ship.x = 350
self.ship.y = 220
self.ship.destination = "Level2"

self.floor4 = Floor()
self.floor4.x = 200
self.floor4.y = 50

...
```

This sets the destination for Level1 to room Level2.

SAVE + PLAY

Similarly, we have to change where Level2 will lead us.

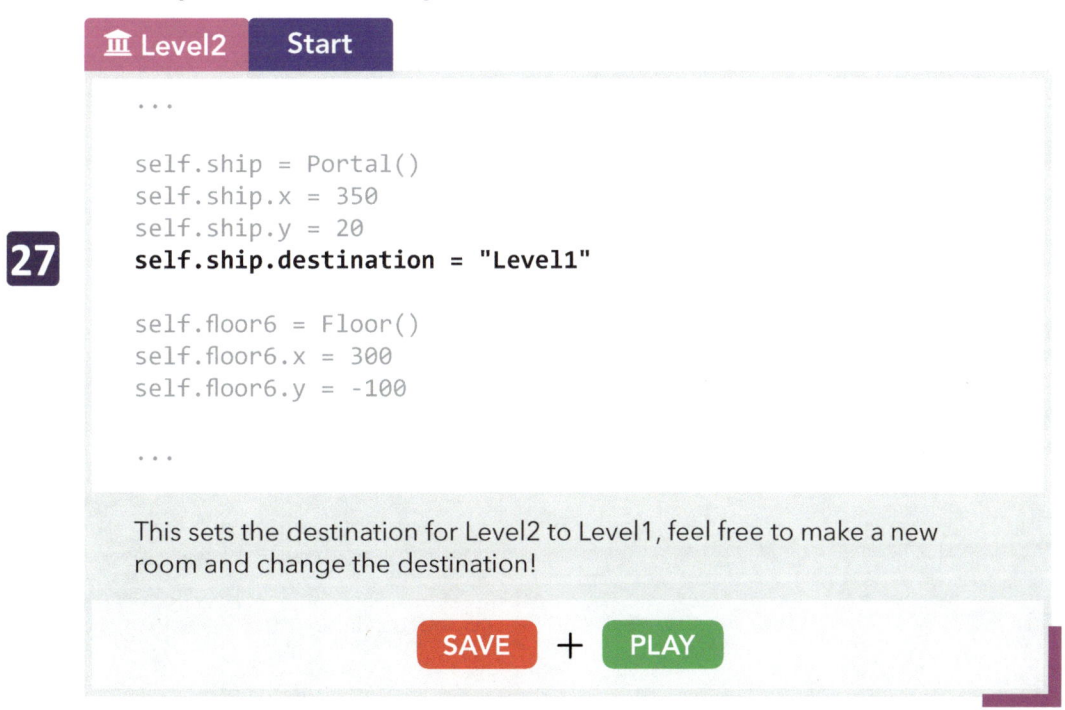

🏛 Level2 — Start

27
```
...

self.ship = Portal()
self.ship.x = 350
self.ship.y = 20
self.ship.destination = "Level1"

self.floor6 = Floor()
self.floor6.x = 300
self.floor6.y = -100

...
```

This sets the destination for Level2 to Level1, feel free to make a new room and change the destination!

SAVE + PLAY

Try it out! You should now be able to travel back and forth between rooms!

Keep going! Try to create a Level3, add floors, more enemies, etc. and make a second portal in Level1 or Level2 that can take you there.

Congratulations! There is now no limit to how big you can make your world. Create more rooms, more portals to access them, and you can go on forever!

09.
CHAPTER

ENEMY AI

We're going to improve Artificial Intelligence (or AI for short) so that the Enemy can change their direction every time they reach one end of the screen.

We'll add some code so that whenever the Enemy flies to either edge of the screen (or close it), it changes direction and flies in the opposite direction so that it won't disappear from the screen.

Enemy | Loop

```
if self.flyRight == True:
    self.x += self.speed
    self.scaleX = -0.7
if self.flyRight == False:
    self.x -= self.speed
    self.scaleX = 0.7

playerHit = get_collision(self, "Player")
if playerHit:
    self.flyRight = True
```

1
```
if self.x > 600:
    self.flyRight = False
if self.x < -600:
    self.flyRight = True
```

Since we don't want the enemy to fly off the screen in either direction, we check to see if their x value has exceeded a certain point on the screen. Here, we chose the values 500 and -500 as our x limits. If the enemy's x value is larger than 500, we change the direction they're flying in to be right, so they don't fly off the screen. If their x value is less than -500, we'll change the direction they're flying to be right so they don't fly off the screen to the left.

SAVE + PLAY

You may want to add other obstacles that will change the direction of the enemy, you can do this by adding another if statement checking for a different object or type wherein you can change the direction!

In the next part, we will make the player and enemy have a health so that they don't die right away

HEALTH

In this chapter, we'll also add health to both enemies and our player so they don't get destroyed in one hit.

Let's start with the player and change our code so that the player doesn't die in just one hit.

To do this, we have to learn about something called persistence. When a variable or object is persistent, this means the variable or object will exist forever, even if you exit the room. All code that is written into the Game script is persistent. Since we want our player's health to be persistent even if we switch between rooms, we will need to write this in the Game Class.

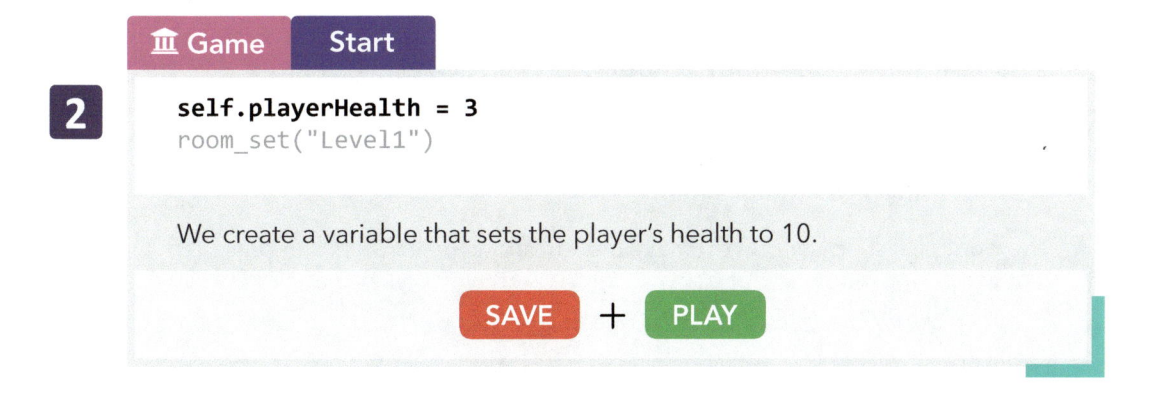

2 — Game > Start

```
self.playerHealth = 3
room_set("Level1")
```

We create a variable that sets the player's health to 10.

SAVE + PLAY

You will notice that the player still dies right away, we still need to change our playerHealth variable, we can do this on the player, and edit the variable in Loop.

Player | **Loop**

```
...

enemyHit = get_collision(self, "Enemy")
if enemyHit:
    if self.y > enemyHit.y:
        destroy(enemyHit)
        self.jumpTimer = 30
    else:
        ~~destroy(self)~~
        destroy(enemyHit)
        game.playerHealth = game.playerHealth - 1
        print(game.playerHealth)
        if game.playerHealth <= 0:
            destroy(self)
```

Here we're getting rid of the old destroy self, this way we don't destroy our player immediately.

Next, we destroy the enemy that has collided with us and subtract health from the Game class variable health.

The print() function used in the next line will show the value of the game.playerHealth variable in our Console window so we can keep track of how many health points we have left.

Lastly, If our health becomes lower than 0, we destroy the player.

SAVE + **PLAY**

Now we lose health for colliding with enemies, and only get destroyed when we have no health left!

ENEMY HEALTH

Now let's set up something similar for our enemies. We don't need the health for enemies to be persistent between rooms so let's add a health variable inside the enemy itself.

4

Enemy | **Start**

```
self.sprite = sprite("wasp.png")

self.scaleX = 0.7
self.scaleY = 0.7

self.speed = 1
self.flyRight = True

self.health = 3
```

Here, we've added a simple variable to store the enemy's health.

SAVE + PLAY

Like our player, we need to change it so instead of being destroyed when they collide with a projectile, they lose 1 health.

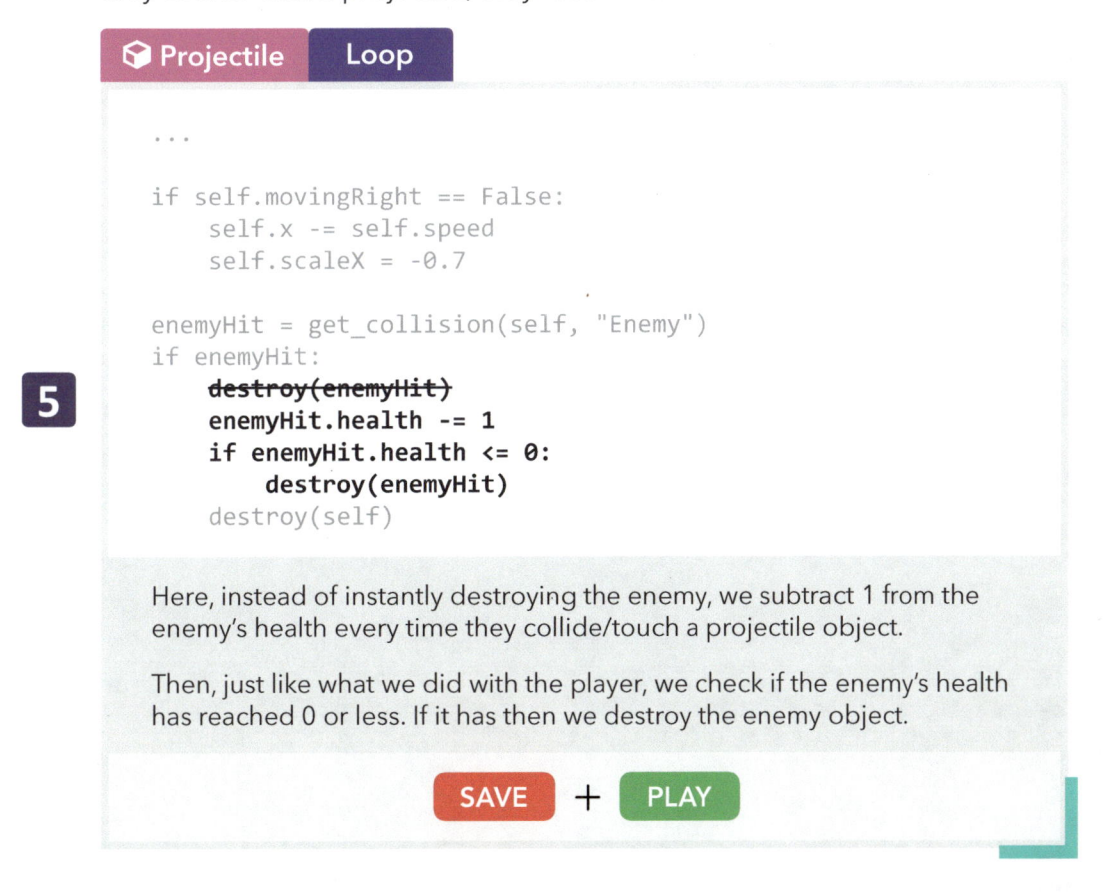

5

Projectile | **Loop**

```
...

if self.movingRight == False:
    self.x -= self.speed
    self.scaleX = -0.7

enemyHit = get_collision(self, "Enemy")
if enemyHit:
    destroy(enemyHit)
    enemyHit.health -= 1
    if enemyHit.health <= 0:
        destroy(enemyHit)
    destroy(self)
```

Here, instead of instantly destroying the enemy, we subtract 1 from the enemy's health every time they collide/touch a projectile object.

Then, just like what we did with the player, we check if the enemy's health has reached 0 or less. If it has then we destroy the enemy object.

SAVE + PLAY

And that's it! Well done for getting this far. Now you can personalize your game and make it closer to exactly the game that you want to make using what we've learned over the past 11 chapters.

You can add things like a new type of enemy, pickups, or new levels to explore. It's all up to you!

Congratulations, you've finished PixelPAD's Platform Course!

Congratulations on completing this course! You can always keep working on your game. You just need to log into your PixelPAD account from any other computer connected to the internet!

SHARING MY GAME

If you want to share your game with your friends, you just have to follow these simple steps:

1. Go to the MyPad Section

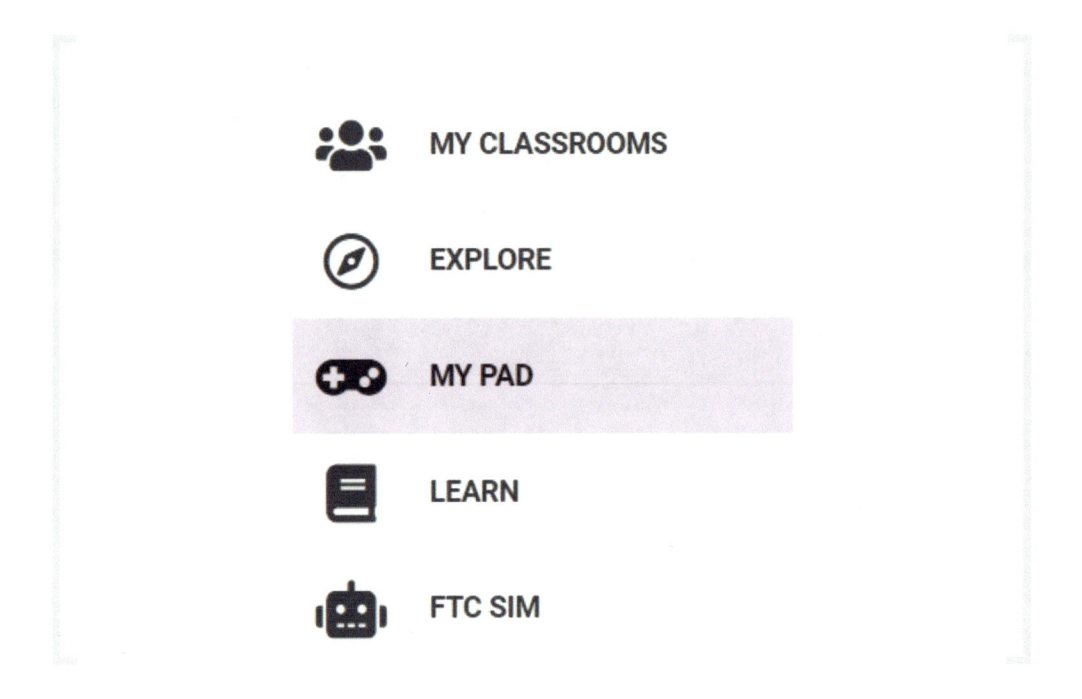

   - MY CLASSROOMS
   - EXPLORE
   - **MY PAD**
   - LEARN
   - FTC SIM

2. Find the game you want to send to your friends and click on the triangle beside the game's name. Then, click Play.

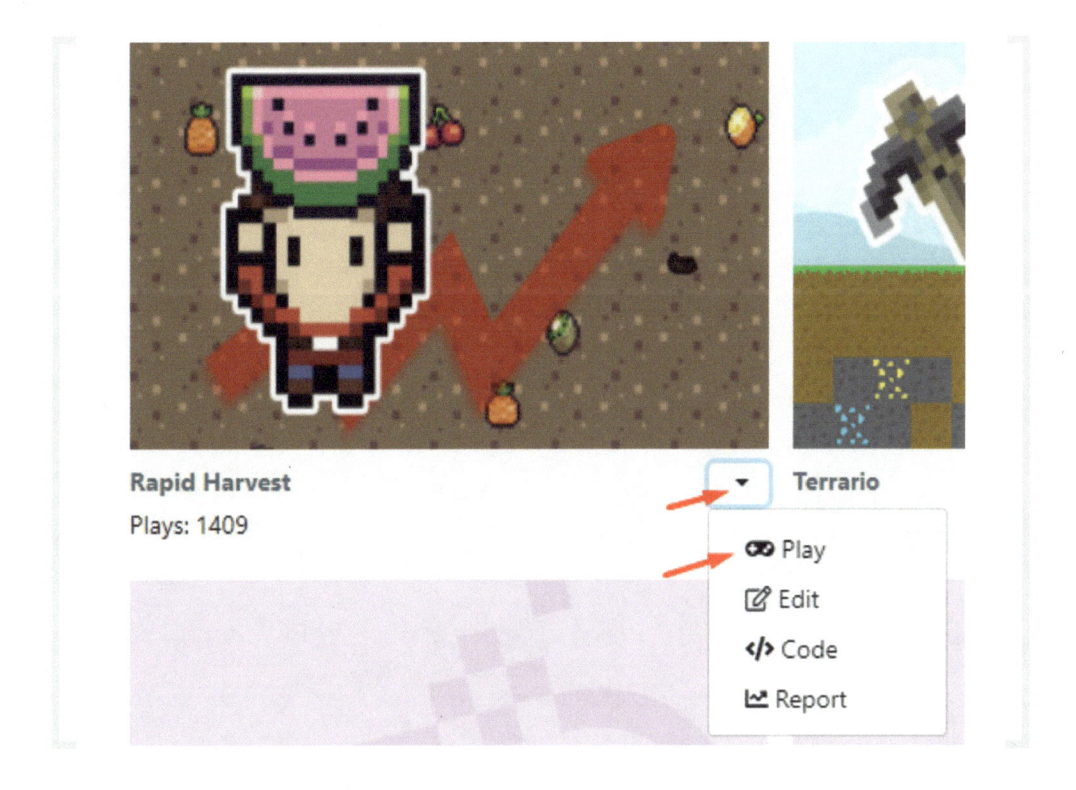

Rapid Harvest
Plays: 1409

Terrario

- Play
- Edit
- Code
- Report

79

3. Now you just need to find this page's link to send to your friends. You can easily find it at the top of your browser window. Simply copy that link and send it to your friends.

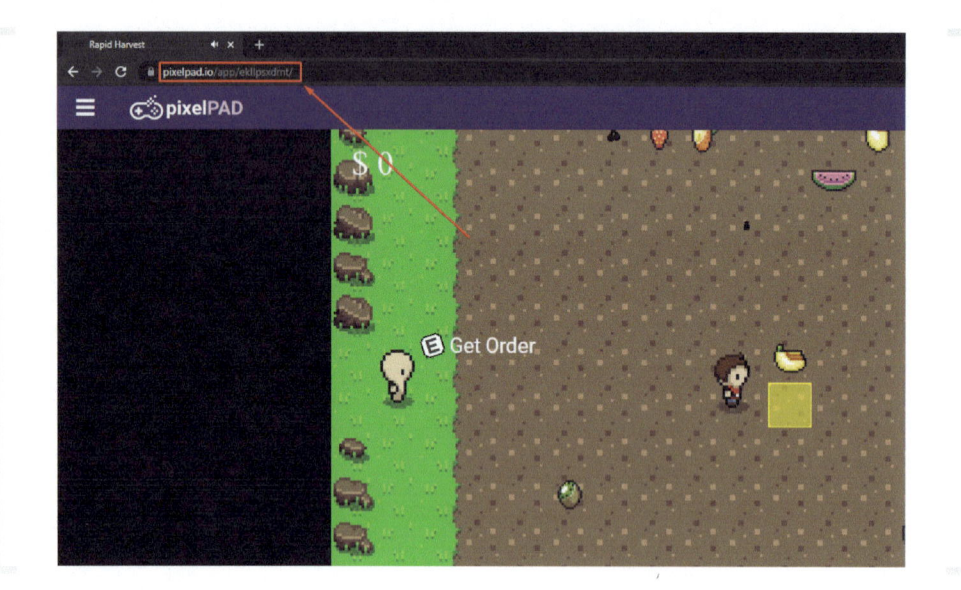

4. Done! Your friends should now be able to play your game!

EXTRA ACTIVITIES

The following activities are optional and should be added to your current game. Most of them can be added during your game's development, but some might require your game to be already completed. You can check the prerequisite chapters beside the activities to know if you are able or not to do it at the stage you are now in the course.

#	Prerequisite	Activity
1	Chapter 4	Create a variable for the player speed and choose a value for it
2	Chapter 7	Create another enemy that moves up and down instead of left and right
3	Chapter 8	Create a Pickup object > When an enemy dies, it always "drops" (creates) a pickup object > When the player collides with the pickup object, the object disappears
4	Chapter 9	Add 5 Levels to your game
5	Chapter 11	Make the enemy to change its direction if it collides with another enemy or a floor tile
6	Chapter 11	Improve your Pickup object added in activity #3 > When the player collects this pickup item, it should increase the player's health in 1 > It should print the new health in the Console

81

GLOSSARY

WHAT IS PIXELPAD?

PixelPAD is an online platform we will be using to create our own apps or games!

The PixelPAD IDE is composed of 4 areas:

ASSETS: Your assets are where you can add and access your Classes and sprites. Classes are step-by-step instructions that are unique to the object. For example, the instructions for how your player moves will be different from the way your asteroid moves! Sprites is another word for image, and these images give your objects an appearance!

CODE: In this section, you will write instructions for your game. To write your code, click within the black box and on the line you want to type on. To make a new line, click the end of the previous line and then press "Enter" on your keyboard.

STAGE: The stage is where your game will show up after you write your code and click Play (or Stop and then Play). Don't forget to click save after you make changes to your code!

CONSOLE: Your console is where you will see messages when there are errors in your code, and also where you can have messages from your game show up such as the score, or instructions on how to play your game.

SCRIPTS

Scripts and Assets

Two of the asset types, rooms and Classes, are script assets. Script assets (or scripts) are assets that have code inside them. Sprites are not considered scripts, because they do not contain any code.

Creating Scripts and Assets: To Create an asset, you start by clicking the + next to "Rooms", "Classes" or "Sprites"

Then type in any name you'd like. My particular convention looks like this:

- "MainTown" -> room
- "Player" -> player Class
- "background" -> background sprite
- "stepGrass" -> steps sound effect

Classes and rooms (scripts) should follow the "TitleCase" standard, where all words are capitalized. For sprites and sounds (assets) we use the "camelCase" standard, where the first word is lowercase, and every word that follows is capitalized. This isn't necessary, but keeps your code neat and readable.

The Game Class

There is one Class that always exists in every project: the game Class. The purpose of the game Class is to load all of the other assets in our project. The game Class represents our entire game.

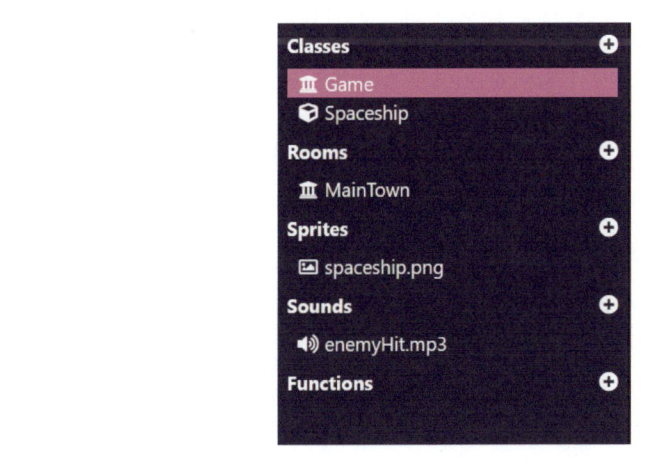

DEFAULT OBJECT PROPERTIES

Sprite, scaleX and scaleY

Every Class inherits default properties when created in PixelPAD. The First of these few properties you should learn about are:

.sprite, .scaleX, and *.scaleY*

.sprite is the image of the object. The value of *.sprite* is an image object which we will get to later. *.scaleY* takes a float between 0 and 1 and stretches the sprite of the object lengthwise. *.scaleX* takes a float between 0 and 1 and stretches the sprite of the object widthwise.

X, Y and Z Coordinates

The position of an object is where the object is. In programming, we usually describe an object's position using a pair of numbers: its X coordinate and its Y coordinate.

An object's X coordinate tells us where the object is horizontally (left and right), and its Y coordinate tells us where the object is vertically (up and down).

[0,0] is the middle of the screen

> .x takes the value of the x position of the object. The higher .x is, the farther to the right it is.
> .y takes the value of the y position of the object. The higher .y is, the higher up the object is.
> .z takes the value of the z position of the object. The higher .z is, the closer to you the object is.

DOT NOTATION AND SELF

Dot Notation

Dot notation is like an apostrophe s ('s). Like "Timmy's ball" or "Jimmy's shoes".

The *'s* tells you who you're talking about. In code instead of using apostrophes we use dots to talk about ownership.

So when we say *player.x* we're really saying "player's x"

Examples of Dot Notation:

> *player.x* -> refers to the player's x value
> *player.scaleX* -> refers to player's x scale (percentage)

The "Self" Property

Self refers to whichever Class you are currently in.

So if you're typing code inside the Spaceship Class, saying "self" refers to the Spaceship Class itself.

≪ Examples of Self ≫

```
#Code inside "Spaceship"
self.x = 50
self.y = 30
self.scaleX = 0.5
self.scaleY = 0.5
```

The code would make Spaceship move to the right by 50px, up by 30px, and reduce its image size in half.

COLLISIONS

What Are Collisions?

Think of collision as checking whenever two objects touch. In Mario, whenever he collides with a coin, it runs the code to add a score.

In PixelPAD, it's when the "bounding boxes" of sprites touch. This includes the transparent areas of the sprite as well!

We will use collisions in our game to determine when our ship is hit by obstacles, when we've collected a power-up or health refill, and when we've managed to shoot down an asteroid.

The get_collision Function

When we want to check for a collision between two objects, we use an if statement combined with a special function called get_collision.

Here is an example of a get_collision function:

```
if get_collision(self, 'Asteroid'):
    print('The spaceship has collided with an asteroid')
```

> - We start with an ordinary if statement.
> - For our condition, we specify get_collision.
> - We then write a pair of parentheses (()).
> - Next, we write self. This specifies that we want to check for collisions against the current object.
> - Finally, we write "Asteroid". This specifies the other Class we want to check for collisions with. In this case, we are checking for collisions with any object created from the Asteroid Class.

BOUNDING BOXES

Sprite's Bounds

Every object has a bounding box, which is the rectangle that contains the object's entire sprite. The get_collision condition checks for overlaps between the bounding boxes of objects, not the actual sprites. This can sometimes create surprising results. Here is an example of two objects that don't look like they should be colliding, but do:

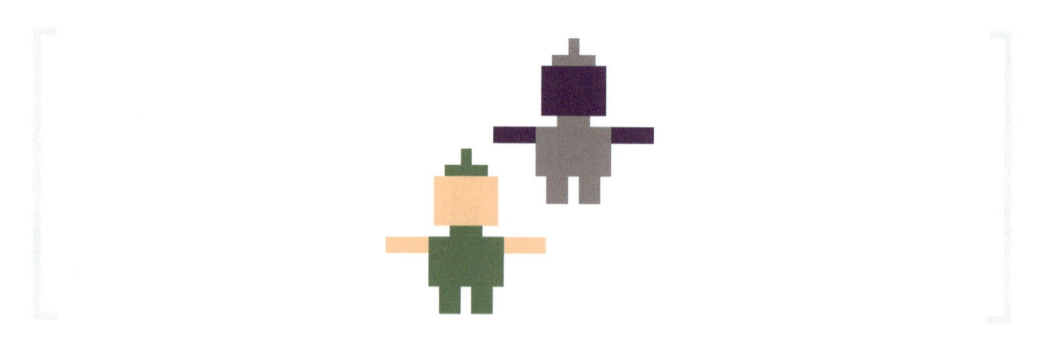

And here they are again, with their bounding boxes shown:

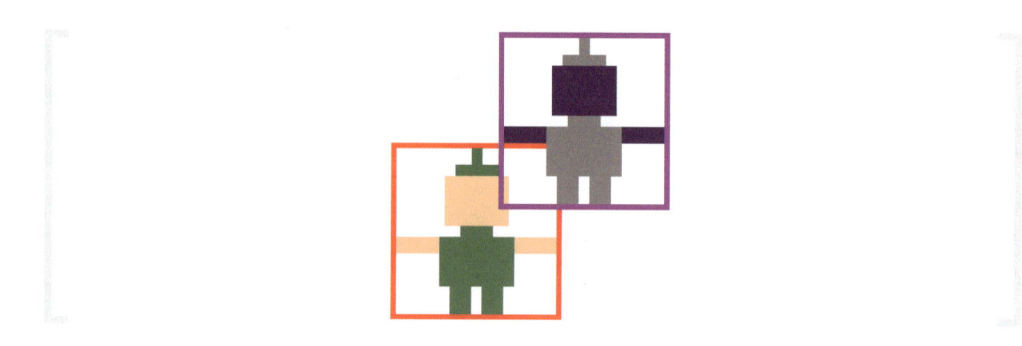

DESTROYING OBJECTS

The destroy Function

When two objects collide, we generally would like to destroy at least one of them. Destroying an object removes it from the game. When an object is destroyed, it no longer exists, and trying to use it could make your game behave strangely or crash.

Destroying an object is very simple. Here is an example of destroying the player object:

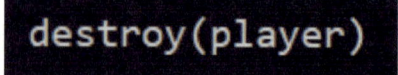

```
destroy(player)
```

THE START AND THE LOOP TABS

Start and Loop

Say you decide to go for a run. You put on your runners and then you run. Running would be the loop because it repeats (one foot in front of the other), and putting runners on would be the start because it only happens in the beginning.

Similarly, in PixelPAD the "start" describes an instruction that only happens once, such as the starting position of a robot. Whereas the "loop" could describe its animation.

The Game Loop

Loops exist in our day-to-day life. For example, you wake up, get ready, go to school, come back home, go to sleep and repeat these things every day! So looping is the act of repeating. In programming, loops describe instructions that repeat instead of having to code each instruction again and again!.

Loops can happen every day, or they can repeat a specific number of times. For example, a programmer can code a robot to jump 100 times, or code the robot to keep jumping forever!

Video games are built around a game loop. Specifically for PixelPAD, our game loop runs the code 60 times every second!

The loop starts when we click the Play button, and stops when we click the Stop button. It goes around and around for as long as the game is playing, updating each of our objects a little bit at a time.

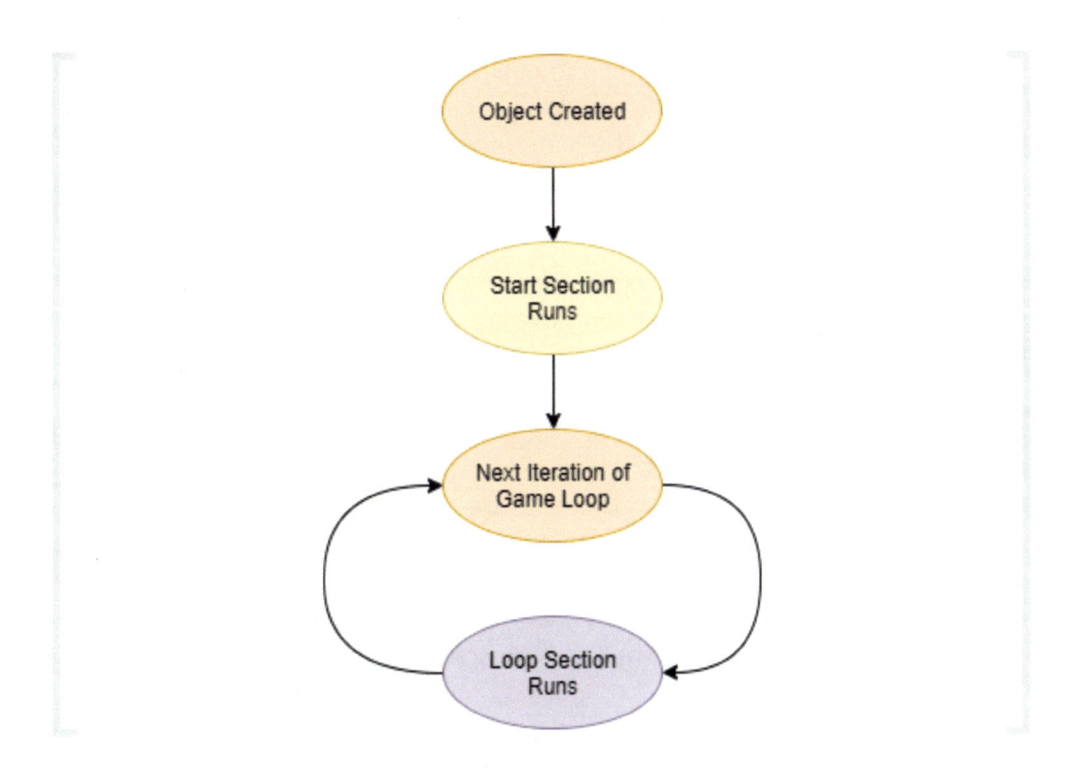

```
Object Created
      ↓
Start Section Runs
      ↓
Next Iteration of Game Loop ⟷ Loop Section Runs
```

How Do We Use The Game Loop?

When we write code for our objects, we can choose to place it in one of two sections: the Start Section or the Loop Section. Code placed in the Start Section is executed as soon as we create the object. Code placed in the Loop Section, however, is added to the game loop, which means it will be executed over and over until the game stops.

CONDITIONALS

Conditions

So far, whenever we've written any code, all we've done is give the computer a list of commands to do one after the other. Using conditions, we can tell the computer to make a decision between doing one thing or another.

If Statements

The way we write conditions in our code is by using if statements. Here is an example of a simple if statement:

```
if key_is_pressed('D'):
    self.x = self.x + 1
```

> - Start with the word if
> - Next, we write our condition. The condition of an if statement is a true or false question that we ask the computer to answer for us. In the above example, our condition is key_is_pressed('D'), which is asking, "Is the D key being pressed?"
> - After the condition, we write a full colon (:), and then make a new line.
> - Next, we indent our code, which means we start typing it a little bit further to the right than we normally would
> - Finally, we write the body of the if statement. If the condition of the if statement turns out to be true, then the computer will run whatever code we put inside the body. In the above example, the body is
> self.x = self.x + 1

INDENTATION IN PYTHON

Indentation

Indentation is when code is shifted to the right by adding at least two spaces to the left of the code. Indentation is important for two reasons:

> - Code that is indented is considered to be part of the body of the if statement by the computer. As soon as we stop indenting the code, we are no longer inside of the if statement.
> - Indentation helps us visually see the structure of our program based on the shape of our code. This helps us navigate our code and find bugs more easily.

For example:

```
if key_is_pressed('D'):
    self.x = self.x + self.speed
if key_is_pressed('A'):
    self.x = self.x - self.speed
if key_is_pressed('W'):
    self.y = self.y + self.speed
if key_is_pressed('S'):
    self.y = self.y - self.speed

if key_was_pressed(' '):
    sound_play(self.shootingSound)
    bullet = object_new('Bullet')
    bullet.x = self.x
    bullet.y = self.y
    if self.powerUp == True:
        bulletL = object_new('Bullet')
        bulletL.x = self.x - 40
        bulletL.y = self.y
        bulletR = object_new('Bullet')
        bulletR.x = self.x + 40
        bulletR.y = self.y
```

We can see clearly that the statements only run if the condition is met. E.g. the player presses the SPACE button.

It is very important that all of the code in the same body be indented using the same number of spaces on every line.

KEY PRESS

Keyboard Input

One kind of condition we can use is a keyboard check. Keyboard checks can be used to determine whether a keyboard key is being pressed or not. We can use keyboard checks to make things happen when the player presses or releases a keyboard key.

Keyboard checks are done using the key_is_pressed function. Here is an example of using the key_is_pressed function:

```
if key_is_pressed("W"):
    print("You are pressing the W key!")
```

The code inside the apostrophes is the name of a keyboard key. Most keys are named the same as the letter or word on their keyboard key. A few keys have specific names:

> - The space bar's name is space.
> - The arrow keys are named arrowLeft, arrowRight, arrowUp, and arrowDown.
> - If you have a return key, it is named enter.

COMPARISONS

Comparisons

If we have code like: x > 300, this is a specific kind of condition called a comparison. Comparisons are true/false questions we can ask the computer about pairs of numbers. There are six main kinds of comparisons, each with its own operator (special symbol). This table shows an example of each kind of comparison:

Example Question	Example Code
Is x **smaller than** y?	x < y
Is x **bigger than** y?	x > y
Is x **smaller than or equal to** y?	x <= y
Is x **bigger than or equal to** y?	x >= y
Is x **equal to** y?	x == y
Is x **not equal to** y?	x != y

There are other kinds of conditions, but comparisons are the kind that we will be using most often.

Adding Boundaries Example

We can add boundaries to our game using if statements and comparisons.

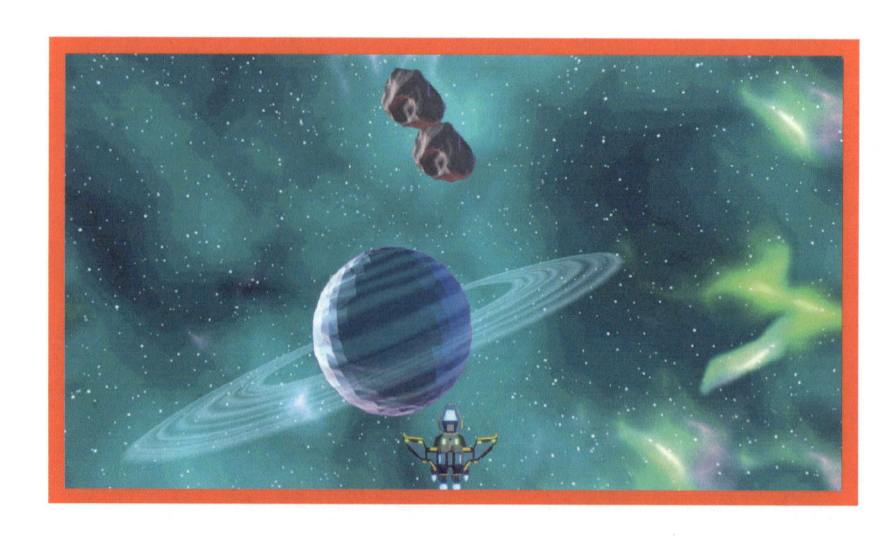

In our Player Class' Loop Section, add this new code at the bottom:

The Left Boundary

```
if self.x < -600:
    self.x = -600
```

The Right Boundary

```
if self.x > 600:
    self. x = 600
```

The Top Boundary

```
if self.y > 300:
    self.y = 300
```

The Bottom Boundary

```
if self.y < -300:
    self.y = -300
```

COMMENTS

Explaining Code with Comments

Computer code is complicated. That's why, a long time ago, some very smart programmers invented code comments.

Comments are like little notes that you can leave for yourself in your programs. The computer completely ignores comments in your code. You can write whatever you want inside of a comment.

How to Write a Comment

You can write a comment by starting a line of code with a pound sign, which is the # symbol (you might call this symbol a hashtag). Here is an example of some well-commented code:

```
# Shoots projectiles if the Space key is pressed
if key_was_pressed(' '):
    self.redLaser = Projectile()
    self.redLaser.x = self.x
    self.redLaser.y = self.y

# Player gets destroyed if health reaches zero
if self.health <= 0:
    destroy(self)
```

Comments are an extremely useful tool, and you should get in the habit of writing them. Comments help us remember what our code does, help others understand our code, and help us keep our code organized.

TYPES OF BAD COMMENTS

Misleading Comments

It's important to remember that comments are notes. The computer doesn't read our comments when it's deciding what to do next. Because of this, comments can sometimes be inaccurate. We should always read the code, even if it is commented, to make sure it does what we think it is doing.

Here is an example of a misleading comment:

```python
# This code moves the player up when the Up Arrow key is pressed
if key_is_pressed('arrowUp'):
    self.y = self.y - 5
```

The comment says that this code makes the player move upwards, but when we read the code, it actually makes them move downwards. If we just read the comment without checking it against the code, we would have no idea why our game wasn't working properly.

Obvious Comments

Another type of bad comment is an obvious comment. Obvious comments don't add any meaningful information to your code; they usually just re-state what the code is saying in plain English. Here is an example of an obvious comment:

```python
# Adds one to x
self.x = self.x + 1
```

Obvious comments clutter up our code and can slowly turn into misleading comments if we're not careful. If a comment doesn't add anything meaningful to our code, it's best to just delete it.

Vague Comments

Vague comments are comments that don't actually explain anything. Vague comments are usually written without much thought, or because the author of the comment was told to comment on their code. Here is an example of a vague comment:

```python
# Grab it
if self.carryingFruit != None:
    self.carryingFruit.xToGo = self.x
    self.carryingFruit.yToGo = self.y + 30
    self.carryingFruit.z = self.z + 1
```

The comment at the top of this code just says "Grab it." It doesn't say what the code does, or how it works. Some of this code doesn't even have anything obvious to do with grabbing. Similar to obvious comments, vague comments clutter up our code and can slowly become misleading as we work on our project. It is better to just delete any vague comments you find in your code.

FRAMES PER SECOND

Frames

When you watch a movie, it looks like you're seeing one single, moving picture on the screen. This is a trick: a movie is a long series of slightly different pictures, and those pictures are being shown to you so fast that you can't tell they're individual images. Each of those single pictures is called a frame.

Games use frames, too. Every time the code in an object's Loop Section runs, the game is drawing a new frame based on where our objects are and what sprites we have attached to those objects.

Every frame in our game lasts exactly the same amount of time: 1/60th of a second. That means that there are 60 frames in a second.

Timers

A timer is a number that counts time. For example, if we were watching a clock, and counted up by one every time the clock's second hand moved, we would be timing seconds.

Since each frame in our games lasts the same amount of time, we can build a timer that counts frames by counting up by one whenever our game's Loop Section is run.

Why are timers useful? Timers let us schedule things. For example, if we wanted an asteroid to appear at the top of the screen every second, we could use a timer that counted to 60 (since each frame lasts 1/60th of a second).

RANDOM & IMPORT

Random Numbers

Most video games use some kind of randomness to change what happens in the game each time we play, to stop the game from getting boring. We can add randomness to our games using random numbers.

Random Positions

For example, whenever we create an asteroid, we've been using code like this:

```
asteroid = Asteroid()
asteroid.x = 0
asteroid.y = 300
```

This code makes asteroids appear at the top of our screen, right in the middle. When we play the game, every asteroid will appear in exactly the same place. We can change this by asking for random numbers when we set the asteroid's position:

```
asteroid = Asteroid()
asteroid.x = random.randint(-600, 600)
asteroid.y = 300
```

Random Function

random.randint is a special command which asks for a random number. The numbers between the parentheses are the smallest and largest values you want to get. For example, if we were writing a dice-rolling game, we could use random.randint(1, 6) to perform a dice roll.

Probability

Random numbers can be used to affect the probability that something will happen in your program.

For example, in the code below we're only creating an asteroid only half the time we used to by adding the random.randint(1,2) == 1 conditional.

```
if asteroid_frames >= asteroid_timer:
    asteroid_frames = 0
    if random.randint(1, 2) == 1:
        asteroid = Asteroid()
```

This code randomly chooses between the numbers 1 and 2. If it chooses 1, it creates an asteroid. If it chooses 2, it does not create an asteroid. Because the random number will be 1 half of the time, and 2 the other half of the time, this code will end up creating an asteroid half of the time as well.

Modules

When we want to use random numbers, we have to write another special command at the very beginning of our program. This is the command:

```
import random
```

This is called importing a module. Since we don't always need to use random numbers, the random.randint command is normally turned off. Importing the random module turns the random.randint command on, so we can use it.

ROOMS & PERSISTENCE

Rooms

Rooms are the big sections of our game. At the very beginning of this course, we set up a room for our game to happen in. Now that we've finished building most of our game, it's time to add a few new rooms.

Recall that when we want to change rooms, we use the room_set command. This command does two things:

1. It automatically destroys every object that was part of the previous room
2. It runs the Start Section of the new room, which should create all the objects that are part of the new room

Because each room controls all of the objects that are part of that room, each room can be used to create an independent section of our game.

Persistent Objects

Persistent objects do not belong to any room, and are never automatically destroyed by the room_set command. Persistent objects can be useful, but we have to be extremely careful to clean them up with the destroy command when we don't need them any more.

To turn an object persistent you can use the code *self.persistent = True* in the Start tab of the Class

ERRORS

TYPES OF ERRORS

Compile-time Errors

Sometimes, we make mistakes when we write code. We mean to type x, but accidentally type y. We accidentally write If instead of if. These are called programmer errors.

A compile-time error is an error that results from the programmer writing code incorrectly. Another way of thinking about it is any error that produces an error message.

Compile-time errors are generally easy to find and fix, because they tend to produce detailed error messages with line numbers and file names.

Runtime Errors

On the other hand, sometimes we've written our code in the correct way, but it doesn't do what we expect it to do. For example, we could expect an object to move in one direction, but it ends up moving in the opposite direction. These are called runtime errors, and are much harder to debug.

Runtime errors occur when code is written without mistakes, but does not behave correctly.

The easiest way to find and fix runtime errors is to use the debug loop. Many problems are caused by incorrect assumptions, so make sure to always reread your code thoroughly to make sure it is doing what you think it is doing.

DEBUGGING

Debugging

Debugging is when we find and fix problems in our programs. Debugging is very important, because it's very easy to make mistakes when we write code. Even the very best programmers need to debug their code every day.

The Debug Loop

When we're fixing our programs, we can always just change code at random until our program behaves the way we want it to. If we're persistent, we can fix problems this way, but it's not a very fast (or easy!) way to work.

A better way to debug is to use the debug loop. The debug loop is a simple process that we repeat until our program works properly. This is what it looks like:

1. First, we Run our code. Running our code will let us observe it, which will show us whether there are any errors or other problems. If everything is working properly, we can stop debugging.

2. Next, we Read our code. Using what we learned from running our code, we look for specific commands that might be causing problems. Sometimes, an error message will tell us exactly where to look by giving us a line number and file name (for example, error in Player.Loop() on line 4 means that the 4th line of code in the Player Class' loop tab is wrong). When we don't have an error message, we have to look for the problem ourselves.

3. Lastly, we Change our code a tiny little bit. Once we think we've found the source of a bug, we can change our code to either make it give us more information (this is called tracing), or we can try to fix the problem. It is important to change only a small amount of code in this step, because whenever we change our code, we risk adding new bugs to our program.

LOGGING IN

Logging onto PixelPAD

We will access PixelPAD using an internet browser such as Google Chrome, Firefox, or Safari. This way you can play and create your game from any computer! Go onto https://www.pixelpad.io

1. Click Login / Sign Up

2. Your username and password will be provided for you! If you don't have a username, please speak to one of your facilitators!

3. Click on Learn, and select the Game Tutorial you'd like to work on. This will create a blank project of a game with the tutorial open to get you started.

CHALLENGE QUESTIONS

CHAPTER 1

What is the difference between the LEARN and My PAD section on PixelPAD?

_____

_____

_____

CHAPTER 2

For each of the following pieces of code, in what direction is the object moving in?

```
self.y = self.y + 3
```

    a) Up

    b) Down

    c) Right

```
self.x = self.x - 7
```

    a) Up

    b) Right

    c) Left

```
self.x = self.x - 3
self.y = self.y + 4
```

    a) Up and Right

    b) Up and Left

    c) Down and Left

CHAPTER 3

In the following code, between what two objects is a collision being checked for?

```
if get_collision(self, "Spikes"):
    destroy(self)
```

    a) **self** and **Spikes**

    b) **self** and **Ally**

    c) **Ally** and **Spikes**

CHAPTER 4

What should you add in the blank if you want to check a collision between self and an object of the class "Fruit"?

```
if collision_check(self, "_____"):
    destroy(self)
```

CHAPTER 5

What is the function to change rooms?

    a) room_change()

    b) room_move()

    c) room_set()

CHAPTER 6

What conditional should you use if you only require BOTH conditions to be true in an if statement?

    a) and

    b) or

    c) !

CHAPTER 7

If our game is running at 60 Frames per Second, how many frames is:

a) One Minute?
_____

b) One Hour?
_____

Bonus: One Year?
_____

CHAPTER 8

What is the library that we import randint from?

```
import _____
```

ERRORS GUIDE

TYPES OF ERRORS

Compile-time Errors

Sometimes, we make mistakes when we write code. We mean to type x, but accidentally type y. We accidentally write If instead of if. These are called programmer errors.

A compile-time error is an error that results from the programmer writing code incorrectly. Another way of thinking about it is any error that produces an error message.

Compile-time errors are generally easy to find and fix, because they tend to produce detailed error messages with line numbers and file names.

Runtime Errors

On the other hand, sometimes we've written our code in the correct way, but it doesn't do what we expect it to do. For example, we could expect an object to move in one direction, but it ends up moving in the opposite direction. These are called runtime errors, and are much harder to debug.

Runtime errors occur when code is written without mistakes, but does not behave correctly.

The easiest way to find and fix runtime errors is to use the debug loop. Many problems are caused by incorrect assumptions, so make sure to always reread your code thoroughly to make sure it is doing what you think it is doing.

DEBUGGING

Debugging

Debugging is when we find and fix problems in our programs. Debugging is very important, because it's very easy to make mistakes when we write code. Even the very best programmers need to debug their code everyday.

The Debug Loop

When we're fixing our programs, we can always just change code at random until our program behaves the way we want it to. If we're persistent, we can fix problems this way, but it's not a very fast (or easy!) way to work.

A better way to debug is to use the debug loop. The debug loop is a simple process that we repeat until our program works properly. This is what it looks like:

1. First, we Run our code. Running our code will let us observe it, which will show us whether there are any errors or other problems. If everything is working properly, we can stop debugging.

2. Next, we Read our code. Using what we learned from running our code, we look for specific commands that might be causing problems. Sometimes, an error message will tell us exactly where to look by giving us a line number and file name (for example, error in Player.Loop() on line 4 means that the 4th line of code in the Player class' loop tab is wrong). When we don't have an error message, we have to look for the problem ourselves.

3. Lastly, we Change our code a tiny little bit. Once we think we've found the source of a bug, we can change our code to either make it give us more information (this is called tracing), or we can try to fix the problem. It is important to change only a small amount of code in this step, because whenever we change our code, we risk adding new bugs to our program.

HOW TO READ ERRORS

Every PixelPAD error is separated into two parts: The error, and the error's location.

```
name 'Playr' is not defined in Game.start() on line 3
```
[Error] [Error Location]

In this case, "Game.start() on line 3" means the error is located in the Game class, in the Start tab, on line 3.

Sometimes the console window won't point to the exact place where the error occurred. That means your error might not actually be in "Game.start() on line 3". If you think the error's location doesn't make much sense, check the last lines of code you've added to your project. That's where the error is most likely to be.

COMMON ERRORS

Name not defined

```
name 'Playr' is not defined in Game.start() on line 3
```

You're trying to access something that doesn't exist. Are you trying to instantiate (create) a class that doesn't exist? Are you trying to access a variable that doesn't exist?

Bad input

```
bad input in Game.start() on line 4
```

Your code isn't done properly. There is probably something missing or extra in there.

TypeError: Properties of Undefined

```
TypeError: Cannot read properties of undefined (reading 'texture') in Player.Start() on Line 7
```

You're trying to load an asset (sprite, sound) that doesn't exist in your project.

<Invalid Type> object not callable

```
'<invalid type>' object is not callable in Game.start() on line 1
```

You're probably trying to set a room that doesn't exist.

Unindent does not match any outer indentation level

```
unindent does not match any outer indentation level in Game.start() on line 2
```

There might be extra indentation (space) in front of line 2.

Object has no attribute 'X'

```
'Spaceship' object has no attritube 'X' in Spaceship.
                    loop() on line 4
```

You're trying to access the variable X inside the Spaceship object. However, that variable doesn't exist.

Local Variable referenced before assignment

```
local variable 'sprite' reference before assignment in
                Hazard.start() on line 3
```

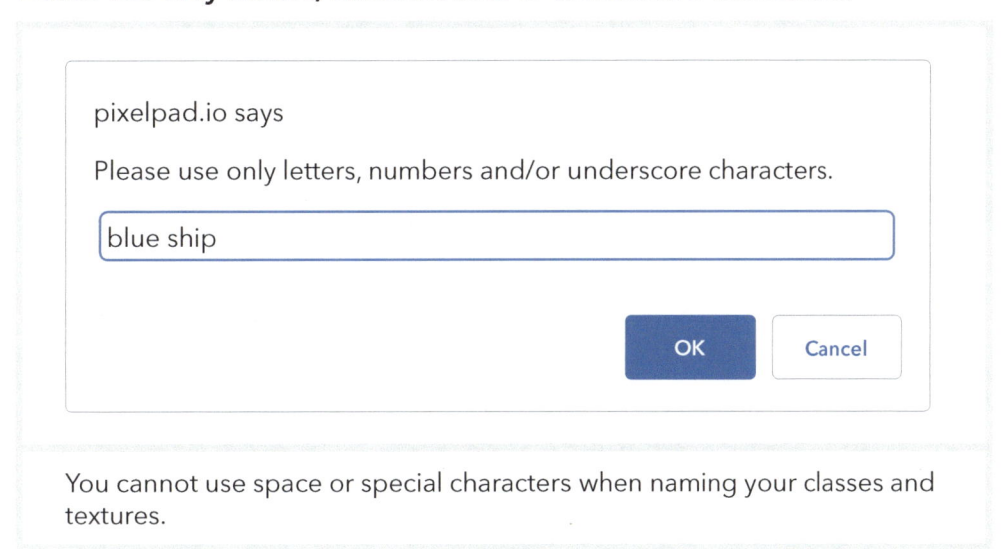

You're trying to access the variable X inside the Spaceship object. However, that variable doesn't exist.

Please use only letters, numbers and/or underscore characters.

pixelpad.io says

Please use only letters, numbers and/or underscore characters.

blue ship

OK   Cancel

You cannot use space or special characters when naming your classes and textures.

Manufactured by Amazon.ca
Bolton, ON